THE
PERSONAL
BANKRUPTCY

ANSWERBOOK

Practical Answers to More than 175 Questions on Bankruptcy

— WENDELL SCHOLLANDER, WES SCHOLLANDER, ATTORNEYS AT LAW —

SPHINX® PUBLISHING
AN IMPRINT OF SOURCEBOOKS, INC.®
NAPERVILLE, ILLINOIS
www.SphinxLegal.com

First Edition: 2009

Published by: **Sphinx® Publishing, An Imprint of Sourcebooks, Inc.®**
Naperville Office
P.O. Box 4410
Naperville, Illinois 60567-4410
(630) 961-3900
Fax: 630-961-2168
www.sourcebooks.com
www.SphinxLegal.com

This publication is designed to provide accurate and authoritative information in regard to the subject matter covered. It is sold with the understanding that the publisher is not engaged in rendering legal, accounting, or other professional service. If legal advice or other expert assistance is required, the services of a competent professional person should be sought.

From a Declaration of Principles Jointly Adopted by a Committee of the American Bar Association and a Committee of Publishers and Associations

This product is not a substitute for legal advice.

Disclaimer required by Texas statutes.

Library of Congress Cataloging-in-Publication Data is on file with the publisher.

Printed and bound in the United States of America.
VP 10 9 8 7 6 5 4 3 2 1

Contents

Part I:
Background Information

THE ECONOMIC ENVIRONMENT TODAY

- ■ Why do credit cards cause such big problems?
- ■ How did we get to this point with credit?
- ■ Why have interest rates caused such problems?
- ■ Why have bank fees become such a problem?
- ■ What is a subprime loan?
- ■ What are interest-only mortgage loans?
- ■ What is a balloon mortgage?
- ■ Is the general economic environment really worse today than it used to be?

Why do credit cards cause such big problems?

As long as you have not gone over your credit limit, credit cards never say no to your request for a loan, and they are always there, ready to play on your dreams, needs, and weaknesses, which is where you can get into trouble if you're not careful.

How did we get to this point with credit?

Credit cards are fairly new. The first general use credit card did not appear until 1950, but credit cards did not take off until the mid- to late 1960s. After that, credit cards grew and grew. Today it is hard to live in America without using credit cards. But the problem is that credit cards, in addition to making life easier, offer instant loans at high interest rates. The charge for failing to pay off your charge at the end of the month became a standard 1.5% per month (18% per year).

Banks found right away that many, if not most, people did not pay off the charges each month, which meant credit cards were hugely profitable to the issuer and a ticking time bomb to the borrower. If a problem comes up where the minimum monthly payments cannot be made, the individual has a ready-made heavy debt load.

People will take vacations, pay for private schooling for their children, buy luxury cars, or redecorate their homes, and put it all on their credit card. Normally, they have every intention of repaying these charges, but it turns out to be more than they can afford. They never could have gone into a bank and gotten a loan from a bank officer for this spending. The credit card, as long as the limit has not been passed, will happily supply the money.

Another use of credit cards we often see is a source of loans to help people out in hard times. When a person for one reason or another (e.g., sickness, loss of job, layoff, injury) loses his or her income, something must be done to replace these funds. Most families have a little something set aside for such eventualities. However, no matter how many assets you have, if the income is cut off long enough, you will run out of money. At this point there is a temptation to use the credit cards to tide you over until things get better. Soon you have no income and a large debt.

Why have interest rates caused such problems?

At one time, in the period prior to World War II, the cost of borrowing money was fairly low, in the 3%–6% range per year. This was true for personal loans and for mortgages. Higher rates than this were illegal in many states, and only loan sharks charged more.

When credit cards were developed, they charged higher interest, but no one expected that anyone would carry a balance for several months, let alone several years. But, as it turned out, many people did carry balances for long periods of time, which meant a lot of profit for the credit card companies—so much profit that over the years they kept trying to get cards into the hands of more and more people. In time, cards were given to college students who didn't have jobs and people with weak credit. To cover possible losses from allowing people who had weak credit to use cards, the credit card companies increased the range of interest rates that could be charged. They also adopted policies of increasing interest rates on individual card holders much faster than for slow pays or other financial sins. Because defaults have stayed rather low over the years, the policy of even higher interest rates on credit cards has resulted in a financial windfall for the issuing banks.

Why have bank fees become such a problem?

Banks have to answer to shareholders, and shareholders want their stocks to increase in value. Stocks increase in value when companies make more money. At some point, banks can't increase interest rates on credit cards or find new people to issue high-interest credit cards or mortgages to, so other sources of funds must been found. Enter the bank fee. Banks have charged fees to talk to a live teller or to use an ATM out of their system, among others.

With credit cards and mortgages, banks charge for paying late. Consumer groups have claimed that the grace period in which to pay has been shortened, that the mailing of reminder notices has been delayed, and the clocking in of received payments has been gamed—all in an effort to collect late fees. Thanks to these and other efforts, bank fees are now a major element of bank earnings.

What is a subprime loan?

A *subprime loan* is a loan made to a borrower who has a weak credit history. The borrower's poor credit history makes loans to him or her riskier, so the borrower is charged a higher interest rate. The term *subprime loan* is normally used in connection with real estate loans, but financial transactions concerning vehicles and credit cards can also be subprime.

What are interest-only mortgage loans?

One type of subprime loan calls for paying interest only. It became popular in parts of the country where house prices were higher than most people could afford. In it the borrower paid only the interest on the loan for a period of time and then began making regular, higher mortgage payments or a balloon payment. The borrower who took out this type of loan was normally gambling that he or she could sell or refinance before the higher mortgage payments began. This was a gamble that didn't always work out.

What is a balloon mortgage?

A *balloon mortgage* is a mortgage where lower mortgage payments— or even interest-only payments—are made for a period of time.

When the time period is up, the entire amount of the loan is due. The monthly payments at times are set at amounts less than what is necessary to fund the loan. As a consequence, every month the debt is growing larger. With a balloon debt, the borrower is clearly gambling on a sale or refinance before the time period expires.

Is the general economic environment really worse today than it used to be?

Yes, it is worse than it was in the 1950s and 1960s. One can argue whether globalization and NAFTA have been good or bad for the average person. But one thing is beyond doubt: it has caused a great deal of flux in the economy. The old, large, stable employers—U.S. Steel, GM, United Airlines, etc.—have dropped employees. Smaller companies, which tend to be less stable, have become a larger part of the American economy. Company-supplied health insurance plans are not as common because the old, large companies have downsized. Defined benefit pension plans have gone the way of the dodo to be replaced by the employee managed 401(k). This may be creating the next crisis—people who don't have enough to live on in retirement.

THE EFFECT ON THE INDIVIDUAL

- Why do people have money problems?
- Why is it so hard to adjust once you are in a money crisis?
- What are the effects of financial pressure?

Why do people have money problems?

We are a nation with a rugged individual ethos. We tend to believe what happens to us is a result of a combination of our own actions and maybe the will of a higher being. Consequently, people facing money problems are often feeling guilt and a sense of failure.

However, in the great majority of the cases we have seen, people have been pushed into their money crisis by one or more of the factors listed below. Perhaps you will recognize them.

- Personal breakups leaving a person with the bills of two people or half the income he or she had prior to the breakup;
- Illness or injury that causes a loss of income and heavy medical debts;
- Loss of employment or overtime and a resulting loss of income; or,
- Age or general body breakdown where one cannot work as long or as hard as he or she once could.

This is not to say that very bad financial decisions or being cheated or misled cannot lead to a financial crisis. But, generally speaking, when one pulls the underbrush away, the core problem in the financial crisis is one or more of the four elements above.

Why is it so hard to adjust once you are in a money crisis?

One of the problems with having a financial crisis is that there is really very little one can do about it over the short run. If business slows down or a person gets sick and cannot work for a month or two, there is little adjustment that can be made in his or her fixed overhead cost of living. Things such as vehicle payments and mortgages are fixed. The only places one can cut back are on food, entertainment, and perhaps clothing. Without an emergency reserve, there is not enough flexibility in those three areas. This leads to a vicious downward spiral.

Creditors will charge late fees and the interest rate will keep compounding as they charge interest on the interest that accumulated from the months before. Quite often before the person knows it, he or she is deeply in debt. What then typically follows is a desperate struggle to keep the creditors at bay. This is typically referred to as *robbing Peter to pay Paul* (paying one creditor one month and then skipping a month while another creditor is paid, dodging phone calls, and getting cash advances to pay creditors). All of this pulls the person deeper and deeper into debt.

Generally, people want very badly to pay their debts. That is the way they were brought up, and they believe it is the right thing to do. They also do not like the feeling of paying their bills in an untimely, inefficient way. Not being able to pay the obligations creates feelings of guilt and failure, and the collection calls and letters add stress. This creates a typical pattern of psychological and physical stress.

What are the effects of financial pressure?

People we have interviewed reported a typical pattern of problems and symptoms when under financial pressure:

- Insomnia
- Sickness and accidents
- Fights with a spouse or partner
- Problems at work
- Headaches
- Avoidance issues
- Depression
- Grief

You may recognize yourself in this picture. People often do not realize how much pressure they are under because of debt until it is released. The pressure built up slowly, and they adjusted to it each time as it built up. But it is definitely there.

They often say such things as, "I'm forty years old, and I've worked hard all my life. I never thought I would be in a position where I was not able to pay my debts," or, "I live in a nice neighborhood and all my neighbors think I have an ideal life. I never thought this would be happening to me. No one knows what I'm going through. I don't know what I am going to do."

Veterans of Vietnam and the Persian Gulf often say having financial problems was worse than being in combat. "I told myself that if I lived through this war, nothing would ever bother me again—but this is worse than the fear of being killed." In fact, some in debt crisis want to die. Many debtors report they have thoughts about suicide.

One very common concern is feelings of guilt and shame. People do not want others to know. They do not want their parents or children to find out they have money problems, and they certainly do not want their neighbors and coworkers to find out. The effect of this is to isolate the individual and to prevent the stress from being released.

They do not realize how many other people have the same problem. There are hundreds of thousands of cases each year moving through the bankruptcy court, and many more cases being dealt with through Consumer Credit Counseling and other businesses handling debt problems. But debt problems are largely a hidden epidemic. Because everyone is hiding their problem, everyone thinks they are the only one to have such problems. The debt problems cut right across all financial strata. We have had many people come to us who had been making $100,000 or more a year and had still almost had their homes foreclosed.

One answer to avoiding financial problems that arise from a cut in income or medical expenses is to have an emergency fund set aside. Experts recommend a reserve of ready money equal to six to ten months of income. While this is good advice, in practice almost no one can follow it. High tax rates make it hard to make enough money to merely raise a family.

Trying to save a half year's income from after-tax money is very hard, financially and psychologically. And if you should do it, what do you do with it? Most people will invest these funds in stocks. When a recession hits, they often get a double blow—they lose their job and the value of their nest egg drops.

If you do have this fund, it will hold the wolf from the door for a few months, and with luck you can get back on your feet. But sometimes it all goes wrong and the crisis outlasts your funds. People who had six- to ten-month funds prepared seem to have as much guilt about having a money crisis as people who put nothing aside.

Section 3

THE DANGERS OF PAST DUE DEBTS AND THE COLLECTION PROCESS

- Can a creditor accelerate my debt?
- Are there steps the creditor cannot take?
- Can a creditor have me put in jail?
- Can a creditor seize my property?
- Can a creditor seize my tax refunds?
- Can a creditor have my wages garnished?
- What should I do about creditor harassment?
- What protection will the consumer protection agencies give me?
- Can creditors file a lawsuit against me?
- How is a judgment entered against a debtor?
- How does arbitration work?
- What happens if I have a judgment against me?
- Can a creditor have my property taken to satisfy the judgment?
- What is a judgment lien?
- How does a foreclosure work?
- Can my assets be seized without court proceedings?

Can a creditor accelerate my debt?

A bank may *accelerate* (ask for full payment of) loans and *freeze* (prohibit any withdrawal of) money held in your account to cover debts owed to the bank holding the account.

Are there steps the creditor cannot take?

Owing money you cannot pay is stressful partly because you feel guilty and maybe like a failure. The other source of stress is from bill collectors and their tactics. When you start receiving phone calls from collections people, they are often quite aggressive, if not abusive. We have been told many times that creditors threaten to have the debtor arrested and put in jail, or to have his or her salary or tax refunds garnished. Creditors often tell people that it is fraud to not pay back the money they borrowed. However, you, the debtor, have legal protection, and there are things the creditor cannot do.

Can a creditor have me put in jail?

One cannot be arrested and put in jail for a civil debt owed to a credit card company or a bank. Normally, the only time you can be put in jail is when you break a law or fail to obey an order of the court in a family matter. Owing money to a person is not a crime and is not something for which you can be jailed. The United States has done away with debtors' prison. Nowhere in the United States can a creditor seize your paycheck or property without a lawsuit or the opportunity for a judge to order it.

Can a creditor seize my property?

Creditors will sometimes say things such as, "We are going to take all your property," or if they are particularly sadistic, say, "We are going to take your kids' furniture and pets." People have visions of their things being taken from their home and piled up in their front yards for everyone to see. This is almost certain to never happen, so try not to let this threat bother you. A creditor cannot just call a police officer and start hauling furniture out of your house. Even if a creditor wanted your furniture, he or she would have to get a court order before invading your home or office. This means that your creditor will have to go through the expense of a lawsuit.

Can a creditor seize my tax refunds?

A private company cannot have the government seize your tax refunds. If you owe taxes or money on a government-guaranteed student loan, then you can have your tax refund seized by the government, but a private company does not have this authority. If someone who is not affiliated with a government entity or collecting for a government entity threatens to seize your tax refund, take this threat with a very large grain of salt.

Can a creditor have my wages garnished?

It is quite common for creditors to threaten to have your wages *garnished* (money removed from your paycheck to send directly to the creditors). This is a powerful collection tool if you are earning a wage. This is allowed in most, but not all, states.

What should I do about creditor harassment?

Given the limited range of what credit collectors can do without filing a lawsuit, they often start by pestering or harassing you to distraction. We have had reports of people getting calls from the same creditor several times a day. Calls start at seven o'clock in the morning and go to eleven o'clock at night. Collectors often call debtors at work after being asked not to, and many times the receptionist or other employees are told about the person's financial problems. Family members are often called and told about the person's debt problems. We have even had cases where collection people talked to neighbors and told them the person was not paying his or her bills.

Books on debt management often advise readers who are having extensive financial problems to contact their creditors, explain the situation to them, and try to work out a reduced payment schedule. In our experience, this almost never works. It may be possible to work out something with one creditor, but if there are several, there are almost always some who will not work with you and insist on full payment. Some will insult you as you pour out your heart to them. Unless every one of your creditors agree to a reduced payment, it's unlikely that setting up a system of reduced payments will work.

The other problem with this advice is that you often talk to a different person every time you call the creditor or the collection agency. You can make an agreement with one person at the agency, and then a few days later get an abusive collection call from someone else at the same company. When you try to explain to the new person that you have worked out a reduced payment plan, he or she frequently will deny any knowledge of it and demand full payment at once. Often they will say, "I have never heard of that person," or, "There is no such arrangement noted in the computer." It is emotionally exhausting trying to explain the same thing over and over again every few days while being abused.

We have heard this sequence of events told to us so often that we are convinced the collectors are using one of two techniques. One is *good cop–bad cop*, where one collector will be nice and understanding and the next will be hateful and try to break you down. The other is the *wolf pack method*. When wolves hunt a deer, one doesn't run up and kill the deer. Rather they will take turns running up to the animal and biting a bit of flesh away. No one bite kills the deer. The deer bleeds to death or just gives up in exhaustion.

People who are subject to harassing collection actions often ask whether there are laws against what their creditors are doing— calling three to four times a day, plus calling coworkers, the family, and neighbors.

The *Fair Debt Collection Practices Act of 1978* (FDCPA), bars all of these acts and is said to offer strong laws regulating the activities of debt collectors. The law bars almost all collector contacts with family, except spouses. It bars contact with neighbors, except to learn a consumer's address and phone number or work address. However, in these contacts the collector may not say the consumer owes money or volunteer the collection company's name.

The collector cannot contact the consumer at inconvenient times, before 8:00 a.m. and after 9:00 p.m., or at inconvenient places. He or she cannot make burdensome, repetitive phone calls or use obscene or abusive language. Work is considered an inconvenient place unless there is no other way to reach the consumer. The collector cannot threaten to file a lawsuit when there is no intent to do so. He or she cannot take any other actions that would serve to harass, oppress, or abuse the consumer. Debt collectors cannot continue to contact you after being told you are represented by a lawyer.

The FDCPA states that the consumer may write the debt collector or creditor that the consumer refuses to pay the debt or wishes to have all further communication cease. If this is done, the only communication the debt collector or creditor can have with the consumer is to:

- advise the consumer that debt collection efforts are being terminated;
- notify the consumer that specified remedies (normally lawsuits) may be invoked; and,
- notify the consumer that the debt collector or creditor intends to invoke a specified remedy.

While the FDCPA bars almost all the collection actions that bother people with money problems, its enforcement provisions offer little help when creditors violate the law. If an individual brings suit, the damages that can be collected are small and proving your case is rather difficult. For this reason, lawyers are reluctant to bring individual suits for violations of the FDCPA. Almost all the cases brought under this law are *class action* (groups of people with similar issues) lawsuits, and an individual's odds of having his or her creditor's violations turned into a class action lawsuit are small.

What protection will the consumer protection agencies give me?

What about the consumer protection agencies? Government agencies and consumer protection lawyers are set up to institute class action lawsuits rather than help individuals.

Basically, you are on your own, and as a practical matter, the creditors can do just about anything they want. There are only two avenues to get help. One is Consumer Credit Counseling, and the other is a private debt manager who, if you can pay enough, may be able to set up a payment program that will satisfy all your creditors. These options will be covered in detail in Section 7.

Can creditors file a lawsuit against me?

When creditors give up on calling you, the next step is a lawsuit. Suing you is not an abusive collection method. You owe the money to the creditor, and the creditor has the right to go to court to try to collect it.

People are often thrown into a panic when they first hear about a lawsuit. Some creditors will describe a lawsuit in such a way as to make people think they will be put in jail. They will say things like, "I'll send the sheriff out with papers."

As noted earlier, you cannot be put in jail for a civil debt. The normal way to serve lawsuit papers is to have a sheriff or other process server deliver them. Sometimes they are simply mailed to you, but many states require notice of a lawsuit to be personally served. Service by sheriff is a favored threat of creditors because it upsets people, and people fear the vision of having a law officer come to where they work or live and serve papers on them in front of coworkers or neighbors.

When the papers are served, they often say that you must answer within so many days, usually thirty. You will not get in trouble if you do not give the court an answer or go to court. It is only criminal court where you can be arrested for not appearing in court. Debt collection lawsuits are civil suits. In fact, there is not much point in going to court if you are being sued for a debt and owe the money. The court cannot excuse you because you have had bad breaks, so going and telling your story does not help at all.

While you are not required to go to court, it is not a bad idea to check with a lawyer to see if you have any defenses against the lawsuit. At the same time, you can get detailed information on what collection actions the creditor can take against you after it has obtained its judgment. A general overview of collection actions is set out below.

How is a judgment entered against a debtor?

If a creditor wins a lawsuit against you, it will be awarded a judgment against you. However, there is another way you can have a judgment made against you.

Most loan contracts today have arbitration clauses that will allow the creditor to avoid the trouble of filing a lawsuit against the borrower. The collection process is started by a letter invoking the arbitration rather than a sheriff serving lawsuit papers on the debtor. The letter notice is much easier to overlook than lawsuit papers. We have had many people who have thought they didn't have any judgments against them, who turned out to have judgments through the arbitration process.

How does arbitration work?
In theory, it works as follows.

1. Either the creditor or the debtor elects to have arbitration.
2. An arbitrator hears both sides' versions of the dispute (this is normally done in a different city than the one where the debtor lives).
3. The arbitrator gives his or her decision. This decision is normally binding.
4. The decision is then transformed into a judgment in the county where the debtor lives.

The debtor community feels that arbitration is unfair because it forces the debtor to give up his or her protection under the legal system, travel away from his or her home, only to have the arbitrator almost always rule against the debtor.

What happens if I have a judgment against me?
A judgment against you may have very little effect, or it can be a disaster. The collection process after a lawsuit or foreclosure hearing is the danger point for any debtor.

Creditors are allowed to take steps to collect a judgment, and now they have a court order on their side. In cases of secured property, the court will direct that the property be turned over to the creditor if the creditor has not been able to pick it up on its own.

Can a creditor have my property taken to satisfy the judgment?

One step creditors take is to have a sheriff take the debtors' property to collect the judgment. Normally, this involves first sending notice to the debtors that they have the right to protect certain assets if they are listed on a form turned into the court within a limited number of days. Because the form is often a bit complicated, and because ignoring the creditor has worked in the past, some people do not fill out the form. This is a serious mistake. If the form is not filled out, the creditor can seize any property the debtor owns, often including his or her home. A favorite target when the debtor does not fill out this exemption form is the debtor's car. This puts maximum pressure on the debtor as he or she needs the car to get to work, and there is a ready market for used cars.

The form normally has different types of property that can be protected. Depending on the state, this protected property area may be sufficiently generous that the creditor cannot seize any property. Should this be the case, the debtor is said to be *judgment proof.*

If your property in a given category is worth more than can be protected, which is often the case for business owners, the creditor can send a sheriff out to pick it up and sell it. At these sales, the property is often sold for far less than it is worth. This amount is subtracted from the amount owed, and the debtor is still responsible for the remaining debt.

What is a judgment lien?

There is another way a judgment can harm a debtor. The judgment becomes a *judgment lien* against land and homes, which means that when the property is sold, the money owed must be paid to the creditor. Land, other than a person's home, can often be taken at once. (It is harder to make a general statement about a person's home. It may be protected or not depending on the state one lives in.)

> **Example:** Suppose Sue owns a home worth $100,000 in a state where she can protect $10,000 of home equity. There is a judgment lien against the home for $3,000. She owes $95,000, so she only has $5,000 worth of equity ($100,000—$95,000 = $5,000). Her home is protected.
>
> However, if she should sell the home, the $95,000 mortgage and the judgment lien must be paid from the money she receives for the sale of her home.

In this example, the judgment lien could be discharged in bankruptcy if the debtor elected to file a bankruptcy petition.

Because of this fact, creditors oftentimes do not bother with trying to take personal assets, but merely wait for the debtor to sell his or her home. They know that almost all buyers will require any judgment lien to be paid off as part of the purchase of the land or home.

How does a foreclosure work?

Another legal process that may come into play is *foreclosure* (forced sale of a home by a lender). Foreclosure is threatened more often than it is done because creditors know it will upset the home owner. Creditors do not really want your home if there is a good chance they can get the money owed them in a reasonable, timely way. Creditors, however, will often be demanding about house payments because they know they have such a powerful weapon to use against you. The foreclosure process works as follows.

1. First, you are served a notice of a legal hearing. This gives you the chance to offer any legal defense you may have. Suffering

from an illness or other problems is not a legal defense. You do not have to attend this hearing, and your time would be better spent talking to a lawyer about bankruptcy because some bankruptcy procedures can stop a foreclosure. But you may wish to consider seeing a lawyer to examine whether you have any defenses.

2. Once the foreclosure hearing has been held, the property is advertised for a foreclosure sale. Because these advertisements are designed to inform as many people as possible about the availability of the property, they can be quite embarrassing.

3. On the sale day, the property is auctioned off to the highest bidder. This is often done in an obscure part of the local courthouse. After the sale is done, there is often a limited amount of time for an upset bid. At the end of the process, your home is no longer yours, and you must move out.

Note: Bankruptcy is a powerful tool to stop a foreclosure. You may not qualify, but rather than lose your home, you should investigate the possibility.

Can my assets be seized without court proceedings?

There are two notable exceptions to creditors immediately filing a lawsuit. One is the *right of offset*. If you owe money to a bank or credit union and have money on deposit there, the bank or credit union can take enough of your money to pay off all or part of the debt. Be careful to remove any money from a financial institution that you owe money to. If you are in a financial crisis with a tight budget, it will be even tighter if the bank seizes what little money you have on hand to pay your mortgage or buy food.

The other exception is the *right of repossession*. A creditor who loaned you the money to buy your equipment, car, or truck can take the equipment or vehicle back if it has a security interest in the vehicle. *Leasors*—those who lend property on lease—can take back leased equipment because it belongs to them. No one else can take it without a court order or permission. If creditors have a security interest, they can take the property and sell it to recover the money you owe them. They cannot use force or violence to take the property and often must stop if you act like you will fight them for it. This is why repossessions are often done at night or while the owner is away. Creditors are not allowed to trespass on private property to do their work, but because they often act when no one is around, some violate this rule. Once they have the vehicle, it is your word against theirs as to where the car was parked.

Once the creditor has the property, it will give you a little time to pay off the loan, and if you do not pay the entire loan amount, the property is sold at auction. The auction sale price is almost always far less than what you owe on the property. You are responsible for the difference between what you promised to pay and what was received for it at auction. This difference is called the *deficiency*. The debt is not extinguished merely because the creditor has the property back—you still owe the money you promised to pay them, less the bit the creditor received at the auction. This is why a voluntary surrender does not help you. You will still be responsible for the deficiency after the property is sold. Often, the fact that you voluntarily gave back the property does not even help you on your credit report. A voluntary surrender is often shown as a repossession on your credit report.

Section 4

BUDGETS FOR HARD TIMES AND BANKRUPTCY

- How does budgeting interplay with personal hard times?
- How is a budget developed?
- How should I distribute my household operating income in order to adequately cover expenses?
- Don't these percentages add up to more than 100%?
- Does the above budget allow for debt repayment above 33% of household operating income?
- How much debt should I have?
- What are common adjustments people make to their budgets when hard times hit?
- How are budgets involved in bankruptcy?
- What are IRS Bankruptcy Living Standards?
- What are the IRS living expenses?
- What are the living expense standards?
- What are housing expense standards?
- What are the standards for transportation costs?
- What are the standards for health care expenses?

How does budgeting interplay with personal hard times?

When household money runs short, everyone knows their family must cut back, but often people don't have an idea of what target they should aim for in each category. Some general guidelines are set out below.

How is a budget developed?

You need to first work out your household operating income. Take your after-tax income and deduct:

- child support and alimony payments;
- student loans;
- criminal restitution payments; and,
- tuition and living expenses for family members at colleges and private schools.

How should I distribute my household operating income in order to adequately cover expenses?

Housing (*Includes mortgage payments, rent, heat electricity, etc.*)	20–40%
Transportation (*Includes vehicle payments, gas and oil, vehicle insurance, bus fare, and saving for a replacement vehicle.*)	10–20%
Food	15–20%
Clothing	5–15%
Recreation, Church, and Charitable Giving (*Includes vacations.*)	5–20%
Medical, dental, and personal care (*If you have a serious medical problem, this could be far higher.*)	5–10%
Debt repayment (*Other than home and vehicle.*)	0–33%

Don't these percentages add up to more than 100%?

Yes. Every family is different. Some will have car payments, others will not. Some will have heavy medical expenses, others will not. The above numbers are a target range. Your family cannot be on the high end of every category, and the more often you are on the low end of the ranges, the better off you will be. You should try hard to always be below the top percentage range in each category.

Does the above budget allow for debt repayment above 33% of household operating income?

Not specifically. If you have to repay large credit cards and personal loans, you will need to cut the percentage of your household operating income you are spending on different categories even more. At some point, you will not be able to cut anymore and will need to consider bankruptcy.

How much debt should I have?

The traditional guideline is that your total general debts (other than house and car loans) should not be larger than 20% of your household operating income for the year.

What are common adjustments people make to their budgets when hard times hit?

What we see is that they will first cut back on recreation, clothing, and food. Then people cut back on medicine and medical care. Most people hold off cutbacks on their children's future, so they are very slow to reduce tuition and college living expenses for children. However, people should be aware if they file bankruptcy, most courts are unlikely to see college or private school costs as an allowable living expense.

How are budgets involved in bankruptcy?

In two ways. When a debtor files a bankruptcy petition, a test, called the *means test*, is run to determine whether the petitioner must file a Chapter 13 or a Chapter 7 bankruptcy. Part of this test looks at the petitioner's living expenses. However, there is a twist. If the petitioner has income above the mean gross income for his family size for his state, he must use IRS Bankruptcy Living Standards.

What are IRS Bankruptcy Living Standards?

The *IRS Bankruptcy Living Standards* are permitted expenses in different categories that the IRS sets as reasonable for people from whom the IRS is collecting delinquent taxes. When Congress wrote the bankruptcy laws, it provided for the IRS expense or living standards to be used in most cases. These are expenses per month.

What are the IRS living expenses?

The *IRS living expenses* are changed periodically, so the numbers set out here may be outdated. In addition, different states—and even different counties within the states—will have different numbers. To find current figures and the numbers for your county, go to www.usdoj.gov/ust/eo/bapcpa/meanstesting.htm.

What are the living expense standards?

Living expenses standards are set on a national basis. Then the size of the family will determine what can be spent.

Family Size	One	Two	Three	Four
	$517	$985	$1,152	$1,370

For each additional person over four, add $262. This expense covers food, household supplies, clothing and services, personal care products and services, and miscellaneous items.

What are housing expense standards?

The second category of expenses is housing. This is done on a state and county basis. Note that the bankruptcy system is different from the IRS system. The IRS system sets an allowance for mortgage payments. The bankruptcy system accepts the actual mortgage payment and allows the petitioner to use it in the means test. This is very important because in many cases actual mortgage payments are higher than what the IRS standard would allow.

However, the IRS standard is still used to control rent payments, utilities, taxes, etc. What is paid will vary by family size. Here are some examples:

North Carolina, *Guilford County*

	One	Two	Three	Four	Five or more
Rent	$853	$1,001	$1,055	$1,177	$1,196
Utilities, taxes, etc.	$364	$428	$451	$503	$511

North Carolina, *Davie County*

	One	Two	Three	Four	Five or more
Rent	$746	$876	$923	$1,029	$1,046
Utilities, taxes, etc.	$370	$435	$458	$511	$519

New York, *New York County*

	One	Two	Three	Four	Five or more
Rent	$3,252	$3,879	$4,024	$4,481	$4,559
Utilities, taxes, etc.	$699	$821	$866	$965	$981

New York, *Oswego County*

	One	Two	Three	Four	Five or more
Rent	$616	$723	$763	$850	$863
Utilities, taxes, etc.	$470	$552	$581	$648	$659

What are the standards for transportation costs?

Operating costs for vehicles are done by regions of the country. If you don't own a vehicle, there is a national monthly allowance for using public transportation of $163.

Operating costs can be by general region or by metropolitan area.

Operating Costs

	One Vehicle	Two Vehicles
Northeast Region	$235	$470
Boston	$225	$450
Seattle	$192	$384
South Region	$201	$402

Operating costs cover all operating costs such as gas, inspections, oil changes, and repairs. These numbers are set using driving costs looking backward in time, so they often understate actual expenses when gas costs are rising.

The treatment of ownership costs is not clear when the petitioner has a vehicle that is paid for, or in the case of a joint filing, two vehicles that are paid for. Some courts will allow an IRS expense for the vehicle, others will not.

The IRS sets a standard for vehicle payments. If the vehicle is being paid for, the petitioner is allowed to use his or her actual loan payment in place of the IRS standard. Often the amount owed on the vehicle will be spread out over a time period longer than the vehicle note. This results in a lower monthly payment in the plan or calculation.

What are the standards for health care expenses?

There is also a standard for health care expenses. It is a national standard, and it differs by age. If you are under 65 years old, the standard for heath care expenses is $60. If you are 65 years old or older, the standard for health care expenses is $144.

Section 5

TAKING A
FINANCIAL
INVENTORY

- What is a debt ratio?
- How can I work out my quick ratio?
- What can throw my quick ratio off?
- What does my quick ratio mean?
- What does a quick ratio between 0.35 and 0.85 mean?
- What if my quick ratio is above 0.9?
- What should I do if my debt ratio is high?
- What is a debt?
- What are secured debts?
- Does defaulting on a home equity loan or line of credit secured by a house carry the same consequences as defaulting on a mortgage?
- My jeweler offered me his company's credit card for guaranteed approval; how does this differ from my other credit cards?
- What are unsecured debts?
- What are contingent debts?
- What are unmatured debts?
- What are disputed debts?
- What is a cosigned debt?
- How are taxes treated in a bankruptcy?
- How are student loans treated?
- How is alimony treated?
- How is child support treated?
- How are criminal fines and court-ordered restitution payments treated?
- How is a home treated in bankruptcy?
- How do I accurately determine my home equity?
- What happens if there is not a mortgage against the house?
- What about other real estate?

- How are one's cars and trucks treated in bankruptcy?
- How is rented or leased property treated in bankruptcy?
- How are personal goods treated in bankruptcy?
- How should personal goods be valued?
- How are tools treated in bankruptcy?
- How are retirement savings treated in bankruptcy?
- What about the rest of my stuff?

What is a debt ratio?

After interviewing thousands of people over the years, we have developed a quick test to determine just how bad a person's debt situation is. For lack of a better name, we call it the *quick ratio*. It is the relationship between your take-home pay and how much you owe, not counting your vehicle and house debt.

How can I work out my quick ratio?

To work out your ratio, do the following (using the worksheet on the next page).

1. **Step One:** Take your paychecks and work out how much money you have each month after taxes, insurance, and retirement are deducted. Money your employer is withholding for payments to a credit union for an unsecured debt and money you are putting into savings (stock purchase, Holiday Club, etc.) need to be added back in. This gives you your *net pay*.
2. **Step Two:** Multiply your monthly net pay by 12 to get your yearly take-home income.
3. **Step Three:** Add up the total of all your debts except what you owe on your house, vehicles, student loans, and taxes. This is your unsecured or short-term debt.
4. **Step Four:** Divide your total short-term debt by your yearly income.

QUICK RATIO WORKSHEET

1) My take-home pay is: _____

2) Add back:
    a) Holiday account _____
    b) Payment to credit union for signature loans _____
    c) Money to savings account _____
    d) Stock purchase _____
    e) Savings program _____
       Total _____

3) If you are paying alimony, child support, or criminal restitution out of your take-home pay, deduct these amounts. _____

4) a) If you are paid weekly, multiply by 4.3 _____
    b) If you are paid every 2 weeks, multiply by 2.15 _____
    c) If you are paid 2 times a month, multiply by 2 _____
    d) If you are paid monthly, multiply by 1 _____
       Multiply your monthly income by 12 _____

5) My short-term debt (the actual debt; not just the amount you are paying each month)
    a) Medical bills _____
    b) Money owed after repossessions _____
    c) Credit cards _____
    d) Bank loans _____
    e) Department store debt _____
    f) Finance company loans _____
    g) Jewelry debt _____
    h) Stereo and appliance debt _____
    i) Loans from family and friends _____
       Total _____

6) Total from step 5 _____
   Divided by total from step 4 _____
   Quick ratio is: _____

What can throw my quick ratio off?

This quick test assumes you do not have unusually high housing, car, tax, and student loan payments. It also assumes your medical expenses and gifts to the church are average. To get a very detailed debt to income ratio, all of these factors would need to be considered. But the quick ratio will give you a good starting point.

What does my quick ratio mean?

- If the ratio is 0.15 or lower, you are generally in good financial shape.
- If the ratio is 0.15 to 0.25, you are starting to get a little too much debt. You should cut back your spending and pay down your debt. See the coverage elsewhere in this book on setting up a monthly budget.
- If your quick ratio is over 0.25, you are showing signs of a dangerous debt situation. The larger your quick ratio, the worse your situation (of course, if your ratio is 0.26, you can fix things easier than if it is 0.65).

What does a quick ratio between 0.35 and 0.85 mean?

Generally speaking, people or couples whose ratio is between 0.35 and 0.85 are sinking deeper and deeper into debt. They may be able to make their minimum payments, but they are not taking care of the underlying debt. Even worse, they are slowly getting worse off. That is, if they add up their total debt from six months ago and their total debt today, today's debt is likely to be higher. Further, without some drastic action, the total debt six months in the future will be higher than it is today. Many people in this situation do not really realize the danger they are in and even think they have perfect credit. They are probably getting preapproved credit applications in the mail.

However, people with this ratio rank are slowly sinking into debt. The fact that their total debt is getting larger means that they, in effect, are paying the monthly payments on their debt with borrowed money when all is said and done. As long as they can get borrowed money from their credit cards or other creditors, they can make timely payments. But, this cannot go on forever. Eventually, even the most foolish creditors will stop making money available. Without more money to help live and pay the monthly payments, it becomes impossible to stay afloat, and a financial crisis happens.

What if my quick ratio is above 0.9?

People whose quick ratio is above 0.9 are very close to financial crisis if they are not already in it.

> **Note:** There are two ways to get a high quick ratio. One is to borrow more money either slowly or all at once. This increases the debt part of the equation. The other is to have a drop in personal or household income. This reduces the income part of the equation. If your household income is cut in half, you can go from a safe quick ratio to a very bad one—overnight.

What should you do if your quick ratio is over 0.9? Make an appointment at once with a bankruptcy lawyer or call Consumer Credit Counseling. There is contact information in Appendix B in this book. Bankruptcy lawyers are listed in the yellow pages or online. You can also call the lawyer referral line of your state bar for a bankruptcy lawyer near you. The state bar is normally located in your state capital or a town near it. (Call information and ask for the lawyer referral service of the state bar.)

What should I do if my debt ratio is high?

If your debt ratio is high, you should begin working out your mix of debts and assets in case you need to file bankruptcy. To gain a rough idea of how bankruptcy will affect you, you must first list and categorize your debts and assets. The bankruptcy court treats different debts in different ways; likewise, certain classes of assets come in for different treatment.

What is a debt?

At its simplest, a *debt* is a promise to pay someone a sum of money; however, in the modern world, this simple rule has been stretched and bent until a large number of items that are classified as debts must be dealt with in bankruptcy. The two main divisions are:

1. secured debts versus unsecured debts
2. contingent debts versus present debts

What are secured debts?

A *secured debt* is one where property can be taken by the creditor if the debt is not paid. The classic examples are car and house loans. If you do not pay these debts, the creditor can repossess the car or foreclose on the home. These simple concepts can be tricky. A surprising number of people feel that loans from finance companies where the finance company holds the car title is not a secured loan. They feel that because they paid off the original financing of the purchase of the car arranged with the dealer and the bank, they do not have a car loan anymore. A loan from a finance company that holds your car title is almost always a secured loan, and they can repossess your car just as fast as the bank that did the original financing.

Does defaulting on a home equity loan or line of credit secured by a house carry the same consequences as defaulting on a mortgage?

Yes. Many people do not consider home equity loans or lines of credit secured by a home to be mortgages. They are both secured by the home, and if they are not paid in a timely way, the holder can foreclose on the home.

My jeweler offered me his company's credit card for guaranteed approval; how does this differ from my other credit cards?

Jewelry or electronics bought with the selling company's credit card are secured debts. If you fail to keep up with your payments, they can repossess the merchandise. A merchant company's credit account often has clauses in the contract that make it different from a true credit card. But, because they are both plastic and the same shape, people assume that both are unsecured credit card debts.

What are unsecured debts?

Unsecured debts are, by definition, debts without property pledged as security for the repayment of the debt. Examples are major credit cards such as Visa, MasterCard, and American Express. Medical debts, signature loans, and utility bills are other examples of unsecured debts. If you owe money on a car that has been repossessed and sold, that debt is unsecured—there is nothing they can take from you.

Sometimes debts that appear secured are treated as unsecured in bankruptcy. Often finance companies, when they make you a loan, have you list property you already own as security—TVs, furniture, etc. In bankruptcy these *nonpurchase money security items* can often be protected by filing a special motion. The test is—are they items you already owned and used to operate your household? What is considered proper to run a home will vary from state to state. Often, sports equipment such as golf clubs or tennis racquets are not considered necessary to operate a household and are not within this exemption. Firearms are treated differently from state to state.

What are contingent debts?

The *contingent debts* are those that are dependent on an event that has not yet happened. A straightforward example is being a *codebtor* on a loan. You will not owe the money unless the main borrower defaults. Another type is the so-called *unliquidated debt*. This is when you may or may not owe the debt. This normally arises in a car accident where you are being sued by a person who says the accident and the damages were your fault. You dispute this claim. You do not owe him or her anything until the court rules against you and sets a dollar amount you are to pay.

What are unmatured debts?

Unmatured debts are debts in which the event creating the duty to pay has not yet occurred. For example, you borrowed money and gave a promise to pay it back in three years. Until that three years has passed, you have only future liability and the debt is unmatured. After the three years have passed, the debt becomes matured. This is a form of contingent debt.

What are disputed debts?

Disputed debts are another form of contingent debt. A *disputed debt* is a debt a third-party claims you owe him or her, but which you deny. There are several situations where this can arise. You hire someone to do work for you, and they do a bad job. He or she claims payment, and you deny you owe them that much, or perhaps nothing, because of the poor quality of the work. Another common situation is where you have paid the debt and the creditor claims it never got the money. It may still be trying to collect, or the claim may only be on your credit report. Another situation is where you never bought anything from the creditor, but he or she claims you owe money and are trying to collect on it or are listing it on your credit report.

What is a cosigned debt?

A *cosigned debt* is a debt where you and another person have both signed for a loan. You are both liable. It does not make any difference whose name is first on the loan. You are each liable for the entire debt. Many people believe that if there are two or three signers, they are only liable for one half or one third of the debt. This is not true. Each person can be sued for the entire debt. It is completely up to the creditor who the company goes after for the money.

How are taxes treated in a bankruptcy?

Taxes are treated as debts owed to a government entity—federal, state, or local. These debts may or may not be dischargeable depending on the type of tax and how old it is. Some taxes cannot be discharged in bankruptcy at all. Two examples are withholding taxes and sales taxes. Back income taxes may be discharged if they are old enough and certain other conditions are met.

How are student loans treated?

At one time student loans, if they were old enough, could be discharged in bankruptcy. Congress has ended this exemption. Now, except for cases of extreme hardship, student loans cannot be wiped out in bankruptcy. Owing a lot of money and having no funds is not extreme hardship. This is the situation of almost everyone in the bankruptcy courts. Hardship is determined by a judge in each case, so results often vary. It often involves a new sickness or disability that would prevent you from ever making the income necessary to repay the loan.

How is alimony treated?

Occasionally people come to us with the bright idea of wiping out their duty to pay alimony in bankruptcy. It cannot be done.

In fact, alimony is so protected in the bankruptcy procedure that some regular debts are deemed alimony and are protected from bankruptcy discharge. It works like this—in the past a person, in separation or divorce papers, would agree to pay certain debts owed by both spouses. Many times this was in exchange for not paying alimony. The trade off was, "I will pay the debts, so I cannot afford to pay alimony." The person would then file bankruptcy and thus end up without alimony or debts. The spouse would end up with no alimony and would be liable on the joint debts.

Congress put a stop to this by saying that such debts were to be treated as a form of alimony and cannot be discharged if the spouse objects to the debt being wiped out.

How is child support treated?

Child support also cannot be wiped out in bankruptcy. In fact, the bankruptcy laws work to force the payment of child support.

How are criminal fines and court-ordered restitution payments treated?

Criminal fines and court-ordered restitution also cannot be wiped out in bankruptcy. The bankruptcy court has remarkably little power to interfere with what a criminal court is doing.

How is a home treated in bankruptcy?

The average person's most important asset is his or her home, both in monetary value and in psychological terms. The biggest worry people who come to us have is, "Will I lose my home?" Normally, they will not. If you look at the exemption charts in Appendix A, you will see the value of a home that can be protected is normally quite small. Ten to thirty thousand dollars is the normal range. However, this is *equity value*, the difference between the *market value* (what you could sell it for) and what is owed on it in first, second, and third mortgages. As long as your home equity is within the protected range, your home is safe.

How do I accurately determine my home equity?

Many people have trouble determining the market value of their home. They first, naturally enough, give the value the appraiser used for the mortgage on their home. Unfortunately, this is not always a true market value. Many lenders have put pressure on appraisers to push the appraised value. That is, they want appraisers to give an appraisal figure that is the highest supportable value. The higher the appraisal, the more likely the loan will go through. After all, lenders do not make money, and their employees do not earn salaries, unless loans are made. The mortgage industry gambled that it would never have to try to recoup loaned money by actually selling the homes that secure loans. The subprime crisis showed this was a bad gamble. If you cannot depend on an appraisal value, what do you do?

Because you cannot depend on an appraisal value, estimates and averages are the next best thing. Many areas are using tax value. Historically, tax values of homes were lower than the true market value of the property. That is not always the case today. Some taxing authorities have found they can raise more taxes by having a higher tax appraisal on the homes and other property in its jurisdiction. People generally like being told their homes are worth more, and those who object to the increased value—and higher taxes it produces—are often too busy to go through the laborious process of protesting the higher assessed value. Thus, over time, tax value has moved closer to actual value.

Another source of information is a real estate agent. It may be possible to have a real estate agent give you an idea of what your house would sell for. Just be aware that many real estate people are by nature optimistic. They may also push the value of the house to some degree.

If in doubt, you can always pay to have an appraisal done by your own appraiser. This is not foolproof. The appraiser can be wrong about the value. Some people plan to hire a friendly appraiser and get a low value appraisal for their home. This is a mistake. A trustee can question the appraiser's value, leading to a trial and great expense. But having a fair appraisal does give you another source of information about your most valuable asset.

What happens if there is not a mortgage against the house?

The bigger problem comes when a home does not have a mortgage on it, either because the mortgage has been paid off (as often happens with older people) or because the mortgage is no good. This does not happen often, but occasionally the mortgage will have a technical flaw. The property description may be wrong, it may be recorded in the wrong county, or even not properly signed. Without a mortgage, the owner will have a high amount of equity in his or her home. If the owner lives in a state with a low home exemption, they face losing their home to creditors or in bankruptcy if they file.

What about other real estate?

This category can cover vacation homes, time shares, and investment property—such as rental homes, second homes, and homes owned for family members to live in. This property, not being the place where the filer calls home and lives, is generally not protected by federal or state exemptions.

How are one's cars and trucks treated in bankruptcy?

As with houses, the exemption for vehicles in most states is quite low. Therefore, if the vehicle is owned outright, and is fairly new, it may be lost in bankruptcy.

People are often surprised by how high the value is on their vehicles in the bankruptcy system. When they seek to sell the vehicle or to borrow money against it, they are faced with a far lower value. The reason for the difference is that in bankruptcy the value is *retail value*. Thus the courts look to see what a dealer would charge you if you bought the vehicle from it today.

How is rented or leased property treated in bankruptcy?

Leased property, vehicle leases, or rent-to-own property such as televisions, stereo systems, and furniture are not uncommon. The right to use the property is an asset, but is normally not one that would be lost in bankruptcy.

How are personal goods treated in bankruptcy?

This is the most elastic classification of them all, including items such as furniture, clothes, jewelry, books, and musical instruments. Different state laws and the federal bankruptcy laws, where applicable, will protect different classes of these goods in different ways. What can be protected and up to what limit varies greatly state by state. To gain a rough idea of what you may be able to protect, you should refer first to Appendix A on exemptions.

But be aware this will only give you a rough idea. Each locale has different twists and nuances. One area may not treat golf clubs or fishing equipment as household goods. Pistols and rifles may or may not be treated as household goods. A pistol for home protection may be a household item, but a rifle that is used for hunting may not be.

Items may move from one category to another depending on how they are used. Art work hung on the wall can be a protected household item, but several paintings stacked up in a storage area may be classified as investment property rather than a household item. Your best guide is a lawyer who is aware of the local treatment of different items.

How should personal goods be valued?

The lawyer will also be your best guide to evaluation. People's natural tendency is to value property at replacement value, or to give the price they paid for the item. But, the court system may allow you to value the items at pawn shop or some other value that is significantly below what you paid for it.

Often the court system will not push too hard on items such as furniture, appliances, and clothing. These are relatively low value items, and as a practical matter, the trustee would lose money if he or she tried to take them and sell them to raise funds to pay creditors. It would cost more in the lawyer's time than the relatively small amounts the items would bring at an auction.

The story is quite different for other items with a ready identifiable market and resale value. Jewelry, silver, baseball cards, and other collections may have high value and be relatively easy for the trustee to sell.

How are tools treated in bankruptcy?

Generally, tools can be divided into two types—those used for hobby or household purposes and those used for business or work (*tools of the trade*). Hobby tools would have to be protected under household goods, if they could be protected at all.

Tools of trade are items you use to make a living. These can vary by state. Almost all states have a catchall rule for tools and books. Once again, valuation is very important. Most people's first instinct is to value at what they paid for the tools. The better course is to value at what they would bring if you sold them in a short period of time—say two or three weeks or in a pawn shop.

In some states, the level of protection can be depressingly low. This often presents a hard choice to the person contemplating a bankruptcy filing.

How are retirement savings treated in bankruptcy?
You may have carefully saved money for retirement over the years. Generally, as long as the retirement program—company pension plan, IRA, 401(k)—is *ERISA* qualified, it will be protected. (*ERISA* is a federal law that regulates retirement plans.) Most pension programs are also protected.

What about the rest of my stuff?
There are a vast number of items that do not fall into the categories of vehicles, household goods, and business tools. Depending on the state, these may or may not be protected. Examples of items that are protected are church pews (Delaware), articles of adornment (Colorado), athletic and sporting equipment (Texas), and required arms and uniforms (Nevada). Additionally, federal and many state exemptions offer a "wild card" that can be used to protect limited amounts of assets not covered elsewhere.

Generally, items such as tanning beds, boats, and campers will be hard to keep, but the levels of protected goods are so varied from state to state that you should always check with a lawyer before making your plans.

Section 6

TRAPS AND MISTAKES TO AVOID WHEN YOU HAVE MONEY PROBLEMS

- What are the biggest mistakes someone in financial trouble should avoid making?
- Why is it a bad idea to borrow against my 401(k) or pension plan?
- Why is it a bad idea to borrow against my home to pay off credit cards?
- Why should I be careful in borrowing from family and giving a vehicle or home as security?
- Why is it a bad idea to take cash advances on credit cards or cash checks?
- Why is it a bad idea to live on credit cards?
- Why is it a bad idea to transfer balances from one credit card to another?
- Why is it a bad idea to lie or inflate numbers on loan applications?
- Why is it a bad idea not to pay income taxes?
- Why is it a bad idea to have someone take over payments on a house, mobile home, or vehicle?

What are the biggest mistakes someone in financial trouble should avoid making?

There are a number of classic mistakes people make when they are facing financial problems—mistakes that make it very hard to salvage their assets when they must consider bankruptcy. The nine biggest mistakes to avoid are:

1. borrowing against a pension plan;
2. borrowing against a home to pay off credit cards;
3. borrowing from family and giving a vehicle or home as security;
4. taking cash advances on credit cards or cashing checks;
5. living off credit cards;
6. transferring balances from one card to another;
7. lying or inflating assets on loan applications;
8. not paying income taxes; and,
9. letting someone take over payments on your debts.

Why is it a bad idea to borrow against my 401(k) or pension plan?

One of the worst mistakes a person can make is to borrow against his or her IRA, 401(k), or other retirement account. It is so tempting. You need money and there is a ready source of funds, often quite large, sitting there just waiting for you to draw on it. The program even has a hardship withdrawal provision.

The problem with this course of action is how these withdrawals are treated for tax purposes and in bankruptcy. Retirement investments and savings are given tax-favored treatment because the government wants to encourage saving for people's old age. Further, there are tax penalties for taking the money out too soon. This is why you receive so little of the money if you simply cash out your retirement account. Taxes eat up a huge portion of the money you draw out. To avoid this, you must set up a repayment program.

However, under bankruptcy, retirement loan repayments are often treated as payments to yourself and are not considered as a living expense when computing what you can afford to pay toward your debts. This presents a *Hobson's choice* to the person who has borrowed against his or her retirement savings. The bankruptcy system, on the one hand, forces him to count the money being used to repay the loan as income. This income can be taken to repay creditors. But, on the other hand, if the income is taken and cannot be used to repay the money borrowed from the pension, the IRS will impose a large tax payment. It is an impossible problem. Better to leave the money in your retirement account and never borrow against it.

Why is it a bad idea to borrow against my home to pay off credit cards?

A close second to borrowing against your retirement account is borrowing against your home to pay off credit cards. The ads are so seductive: "Pay off your high interest credit cards with a lower interest second (or third or fourth) loan against your home. The interest payments may even be tax deductible." More and more people are taking this step to settle their short-term debt concerns. But it can be a big mistake. You are trading debts you can discharge in bankruptcy for a debt that you must pay to avoid losing your home.

A person's home is the queen of his or her property. Almost everyone who is considering bankruptcy says first, "I don't care what else I lose; I want to save my home." A house means shelter for one's family, but it's so much more than that. It is the receptacle for one's dreams and often how one defines oneself to the world. In fact, one of the reasons people do not look into bankruptcy sooner is a general perception that people who file for bankruptcy inevitably lose their homes.

This often does not happen, but it can. To avoid losing your home, planning in borrowing can be very important. Almost every state allows a person to keep a home, providing he or she does not have too much equity in the house (the value of the house less what is owed on it). How much equity you can have will vary by state. In New York, it is $50,000. In New Jersey, there is no state exemption but one can use the federal exemption of $20,200. Some states—notably Florida and Texas—allow unlimited exemptions (but do limit the size of the property).

If you have equity in your home over the allowed maximum, you run the risk of losing your home. The trustee can sell it, give you the protected equity, and distribute the balance of the sale proceeds to your creditors. The trustee will typically give you the chance to buy the house first at the price he would likely receive from the sale, but you normally cannot come up with a large amount of money when filing bankruptcy.

One way to avoid the problem is to have more debt on your home. Ironically, in this situation, it may make sense to borrow against your home in order to pay off your debts. If you can weather your financial storm by reducing your credit card payments, and move your house equity into the protected zone, this borrowing strategy may pay off, but only in a planned, logical way. To do this you need to know three things:

1. The home exemption in force in your state. (You can get a general idea by looking at Appendix A, but do not rely solely on it. States change their exemption levels constantly and any printed book runs the risk of being out of date; check with a bankruptcy lawyer.)

2. How much you owe on your home. (A simple call to your mortgage holder for the payoff will gather this information.)
3. The value of your home.

This is not as simple as it seems. Most people, when asked for the value of their home, will give the appraisal value. Historically, this made sense, as banks wanted their appraisals to be concrete. Today, lenders are more interested in having the loan go through. To do this, they need a good house value. The lending industry is now putting pressure on appraisers to push the house values—to give it the highest plausible value.

The problem is that these artificially pushed values often are unrealistic when it comes to selling the house, particularly if the sale is to be soon after the appraisal. In your planning, you might as well collect a realistic value for the house. Normally, this is a blending of real estate agents' values (remember these also are often high), the appraisal value, and the tax value. It is well worth paying a bankruptcy lawyer to discuss with you what the local legal bankruptcy culture on house value is before making your borrowing plans. You may even want to hire your own appraiser and tell him or her not to artificially push the value. You are working with your most precious asset, and you do not want to be flying blind when making your plans.

When you have these numbers, it makes sense to borrow up to the line of your state exemption, and no further. If your state exemption is $10,000 and your home has $30,000 in equity, borrow $20,000 against your home and pay down other bills. This way you may weather your financial problems.

Sometimes it makes sense to borrow against your home to pay back what you borrowed from your 401(k) or retirement plan. As noted above, loans from retirement programs hurt you if it comes to bankruptcy and loans against extra equity in your house, within limits, can help you save your home.

Within limits is a key term. It does not do you a bit of good to borrow against your home if you cannot make the monthly payments. Whether it is called a second mortgage or a home equity loan, it still has your house as collateral. As such you will lose your home to foreclosure if you do not make the monthly payments. (It is amazing how many people, when asked to list the mortgages against their home, will not list a home equity line. Somehow the difference in name fools them.)

Why should I be careful in borrowing from family and giving a vehicle or home as security?

After reviewing the problems of borrowing against a vehicle or home, people often go to family and friends and borrow money. They give their car title or promise their home as security for the loan. The lender in such a friendly loan situation will either hold their car title or have their name listed as a lien holder on the title. If it is a loan against the home, they will draw up a note themselves and list the home as collateral for the loan. Such informal loans and security actions almost never hold up in bankruptcy court. The trustee sets aside the lender's claim, and the vehicle or home is treated as if nothing was owed on it.

If someone is going to lend you money with your vehicle or home as security, take the time to put the transaction on a formal basis with the proper security documents. It is better to spend a little money to have a lawyer do the paperwork than to lose your home or vehicle. And remember, if the documents are not correct, your family member may have to give back the loan payments because the courts consider it an insider preference. Once the loan is formally set up, be sure to make the monthly payment. The loan may be voided if you don't.

Why is it a bad idea to take cash advances on credit cards or cash checks?

As money pressures mount, people often turn to whatever credit they can gain to keep themselves going. Common sources are credit cards, large cash advances, or the checks creditors send to people in the mail. These last-resort measures create a spike in your borrowing pattern. This can be used against you.

There once was a time when if a creditor extended you credit and you were not able to repay it, that was the creditor's problem. But, over the years, the credit card companies were able to convince the courts that such debts should not be discharged. Credit card companies started looking for anything that looked like a spending spree, such as a large charge in a short period of time. Requesting a large cash advance or cashing a mailed check will be treated the same as a glut of spending on a Las Vegas vacation. Often the credit card company will attack first and try to put the burden on you to demonstrate you were not trying to defraud them. This aggressive action by the credit card industry when you take cash advances or cash checks can make your bankruptcy more expensive, as you may have to defend yourself in bankruptcy court and may even lose if the judge does not think you acted properly. The best advice is not to suddenly change your charging habits.

Why is it a bad idea to live on credit cards?

If you are using a credit card to tide you over the rough spots, you should be reasonable. You must make a realistic assessment of when there is no hope of turning your finances around. If it goes to court or is challenged by the credit card company, the judge will make an assessment of your judgment and whether you should have thought you had a realistic chance of repaying the money you were borrowing on the credit card. If you used your credit cards with no reasonable intent of paying them back, the court may not allow those debts to be discharged.

Why is it a bad idea to transfer balances from one credit card to another?

Sometimes advice you are given about trying to work yourself out of debt can come back to harm you. One bit of advice you often hear is to move debt from a high interest credit card to a lower interest credit card. This helps by reducing the amount you must pay each month, and in theory makes it easier for you to pay off your debts.

The problem with this strategy in the bankruptcy context is that it creates the same type of spike on the new lower interest credit cards that a cash advance or Las Vegas trip would. And even though the credit card company encouraged you to take this action in their promotional literature, they may turn around and attack you for bankruptcy fraud. You will be faced with the expense and worry of responding to their claims and accusations.

Again, the best safeguard against this type of problem is sober judgment. You must step back and make an assessment as to whether or not making such a balance transfer will really help or whether you are merely rearranging the deck chairs on the *Titanic*.

Why is it a bad idea to lie or inflate numbers on loan applications?

Bankruptcy has a way of making small lies about your income or your assets on loan applications blow up in your face. It's an easy trap to fall into. People misvalue their assets all the time, with varying degrees of guilt. When applying for a large loan, you often have to produce income tax records; people will make the case that their worth is greater than reported, and the loan officer, eager to close the deal, will accept the explanation. The potential borrower may give the insured value or even the replacement value for personal items. Often this is done with the acquiescence or even the pushing of the loan officer. One story heard fairly often is that a loan officer will tell the would-be-borrower, "You don't have enough asset value to qualify for the loan; think again about your goods and their value." Some loan officers even go through the application and systematically mark up given values.

All of this blows up when a bankruptcy petition is filed. The income is lower and is not based on predictions but on cold, depressing facts. The values of goods and property are listed at far lower, forced sale values. The relatively friendly and helpful loan officer disappears. In her place comes a stern recovery officer waving the loan application and implying fraud by the borrower. These differences can be very hard to explain even if the difference is the innocent *puffing-up of numbers* when applying for the loan. It can be far worse if you actually lied.

At best, loans made on the basis of your fraud are not dischargeable, and at worst you may face criminal charges of fraud. Never lie on a loan application. Always try to put a fair value on your assets and do not let the loan taker put down information that is not correct. The same set of statements are always made: "I didn't say/write that!" and "That's your signature, isn't it?"

Why is it a bad idea not to pay income taxes?

When you are having money problems, a seemingly easy source of money is the government. People simply do not pay their taxes. It takes every bit of money they have to stay afloat, and at year end they have nothing they can send to the government.

This is a big mistake. The IRS may be acting nicer of late, but they are still a very hard organization to deal with. Taxes are a necessary, integral part of life, and if you cannot afford to pay them, you should take a hard look at your life and make adjustments.

Note: File a tax return even if you cannot pay your taxes for the year or do not believe you owe any because of low income or losses.

In certain cases it is possible to completely discharge taxes in a bankruptcy. The rules are complex, but basically the taxes must be old ones and you must have filed your tax returns. If you do not file your return, you are not eligible for this limited chance at a complete discharge.

When it comes time to deal with your late taxes, they will be much higher than the simple amount you owed for a given tax year. The IRS will add interest and penalties, which can be quite devastating.

Why is it a bad idea to have someone take over payments on a house, mobile home, or vehicle?

Occasionally we will interview people who, in an effort to sell a home or vehicle, will reach an agreement with a third party to have that person take over the payments on the seller's house, mobile home, or vehicle. The collateral will be transferred into the third party's name when it is paid off.

This is a bad idea for both parties. If the buyer doesn't have a written contract, he is making payments of collateral that is legally in another person's name, and that person may not put the property in the payor's name when all the payments have been made.

From the seller's point of view, this is not a real sale, and the seller's name has not been taken off the debt. If the buyer doesn't make the required payments, it will go against the seller's credit.

Section 7

WHAT WILL I LOSE?

- Will I lose everything if I file bankruptcy?
- Who can take my property?
- What can secured creditors take from me?
- What can the trustee take from me?
- How does owning property with no debt against it hurt me in bankruptcy?

Will I lose everything if I file bankruptcy?

There is a widespread belief that you will lose all your property if you file bankruptcy. This is often not the case. There are ways to predict what you might lose and how to make an assessment of what is at risk.

What is protected in bankruptcy and what is lost will depend in large part on what state you live in. Appendix A gives a state-by-state breakdown of levels of protection in the different states.

Who can take my property?

In looking to see what will be lost in bankruptcy, it should be remembered that after you file, two sets of people have an interest in your property. First, there is the trustee whose duty is to collect property that is not exempt and sell it for the benefit of your creditors. The state exemptions set out what is exempt or protected from the trustee. The second group is the *secured creditor*. These are entities such as mortgage holders on your home or lien holders on your cars and trucks.

What can secured creditors take from me?

If secured creditors are not paid, they can repossess your home or vehicle. Often a trustee will not be interested in property because more is owed on it than it is worth. This means the trustee would not make any money from the general creditors if the property were seized and sold. So the trustee does not bother with the property.

What can the trustee take from me?

Let's take two individuals, Sue and Tom, and see how they would be treated in three different states—North Carolina, Texas, and Tennessee.

SUE:

Sue has limited what she has bought over the years. She has one child, age 10, who loves to ride horses. Her one luxury is a horse for the child to ride after school and on weekends. Sue has personal debts of $70,000 and has the following property.

EQUITY

1. A home with a market value of $100,000. $0
    The first and second mortgages total $102,000.   (100,000—102,000)
2. An SUV worth $26,000. She owes $27,000 on it. $0
                                                        (26,000—27,000)
3. A second vehicle worth $3,000. $3,000
4. Tools and equipment worth $2,000, used in a
    business she operates. $2,000
5. Household furnishings and clothes worth $4,000. $4,000
6. A 401(k) with $50,000 in stock. $50,000
7. A horse worth $1,500. $1,500

TOM:

Tom has spent more than Sue and owns property worth more than Sue. Tom also has one child, age 10, who loves to ride horses. His one luxury is a horse for the child to ride after school and on weekends. Tom has debts of $140,000 and has the following property.

EQUITY

1. A home with a market value of $200,000. $155,000
    The first and second mortgages on the home
    equal $45,000.   (200,000—45,000)

2. An SUV worth $26,000. He owes $16,000 on it. $10,000
                                                           (26,000—16,000)
3. A second vehicle worth $3,000. $3,000
4. Tools and equipment worth $4,000, used in a business
    he operates. $4,000
5. Household furnishings and clothes worth $8,000. $8,000
6. A 401(k) with $100,000 in stock. $100,000
7. A horse worth $3,000. $3,000

How these two people are treated in a Chapter 7 bankruptcy will differ greatly in our three sample states.

SUE:

NORTH CAROLINA

The applicable property values that can be protected (not used for bankruptcy and left with the debtor) in North Carolina are as follows:

Home Equity	$18,500
Car Equity (for one car)	$3,500
Work Tools and Equipment	$2,000
Household Goods	$5,000
Extra protection of household goods for each dependent	$1,000
A wild card of $5,000 of home equity not used (the wild card can be used to protect anything)	$5,000

In North Carolina, Sue will have her property treated as follows:

Home	Can Keep. There is no equity in the home, so the trustee will not take it to sell for the benefit of the creditors. Sue will need to continue to pay the first and second mortgages to protect her home from the mortgage holders.
SUV	Can Keep. There is no equity in the car, so the trustee will not take it to sell for the benefit of the creditors. Sue will need to continue to pay the lien holder to protect the SUV.
Second Vehicle	Protected. The vehicle protection of $3,500 can be applied against this.
Work Tools and Equipment	Protected.
Household Goods	Protected.
Stock in 401(k)	Protected.
Horse	Not fully protected. Sue can use $1,500 of her wild card to protect the value of the horse.

TEXAS

In Texas, the property values that can be protected are as follows:

Home Equity	Unlimited
Miscellaneous (can protect home furnishings, clothes, one motor vehicle, tools of the trade, and two horses)	$60,000

In Texas, Sue will have her property treated as follows:

Home	Can Keep. There is no equity in the home, so the trustee will not take it to sell for the benefit of the creditors. Sue will need to continue to pay the first and second mortgages to protect her home from the mortgage holders.
SUV	Can Keep. There is no equity in the car, so the trustee will not take it to sell for the benefit of the creditors. Sue will need to continue to pay the lien holder to protect the SUV.
Second Vehicle	Protected. Sue would use her one car protection for this vehicle as part of her general $60,000 exemption.
Work Tools and Equipment	Protected. Part of her $60,000 exemption.
Household Goods	Protected. Part of her $60,000 exemption.
Stock in 401(k)	Protected.
Horse	Protected. Part of her $60,000 exemption.

TENNESSEE

In Tennessee, the applicable property values that can be protected are as follows:

Home Equity	$5,000 for a single person
Vehicle Equity	Included under Household Goods.
Work Tools and Equipment	$1,950
Household Goods	$4,000. In addition, all clothing, school books, pictures, portraits, and a bible.

The result for Sue in Tennessee is as follows:

Home	Can Keep. There is no equity in the home, so the trustee will not take it to sell for the benefit of the creditors. Sue will need to continue to pay the first and second mortgages to protect her home from the mortgage holders.
SUV	Can Keep. There is no equity in the car, so the trustee will not take it to sell for the benefit of the creditors. Sue will need to continue to pay the lien holder to protect the SUV.
Second Vehicle	Can protect the car by using $3,000 from the $4,000 household goods exemption.
Work Tools and Equipment	Can protect $1,950 of the $2,000 value.
Household Goods	Can protect all of her clothes and any of the $4,000 household goods exemption not used to protect the second car.
Stock in 401(k)	Protected.
Horse	Not protected.

TOM:

How would Tom be treated in the different states? Tom owes more money and has property of a higher value than Sue.

NORTH CAROLINA

How will Tom be treated in North Carolina?

Home	Not protected. The $155,000 in equity is far larger than the $18,500 protected zone.
SUV	Not protected. The $10,000 in equity is larger than the $3,500 vehicle protected zone can provide, even if the wild card was added to it.
Second Vehicle	Protected. The $3,500 vehicle protection can be applied successfully here.
Work Tools and Equipment	Partly protected. $2,000 worth is protected by the work tool exemption, and if the house is given up, he can use the wild card to exempt the other $2,000.
Household Goods	Partly protected. Tom can protect $5,000 worth of household goods and his child can protect $1,000. The remaining balance can be protected by using part of the wild card if he gives up his house and if he doesn't use the Wild Card for other property.
Stock in 401(k)	Protected.
Horse	Not fully protected. Tom can use $1,000 of his remaining wild card to protect part of the value of the horse if he gives up his house.

TEXAS

How will Tom be treated in Texas?

Home	Protected.
SUV	Protected. Part of his $60,000 exemption.
Second Vehicle	Not protected. He can only protect one vehicle.
Work Tools and Equipment	Protected. Part of his $60,000 exemption.
Household Goods	Protected. Part of his $60,000 exemption.
Stock in 401(k)	Protected.
Horse	Protected. Part of his $60,000 exemption.

TENNESSEE

How will Tom be treated in Tennessee?

Home	Not protected.
SUV	Not protected.
Second Vehicle	Can protect the second car by using $3,000 of the $4,000 from the household goods exemption.
Work Tools and Equipment	Can protect $1,950 of the $4,000 value.
Household Goods	Can protect his clothes and up to $4,000 (assuming the second car was not protected) of household furnishings.
Stock in 401(k)	Protected.
Horse	Not protected.

How does owning property with no debt against it hurt me in bankruptcy?

A few observations are in order. The result did not depend on the size of the unsecured debt. But it did vary on the amount of secured debt against homes and vehicles. In our example, clearly Texas is the best place to live if you have to file bankruptcy, and Tennessee is the worst place to file.

Texas and Ohio are extreme examples. Most states fall somewhere in between. The states vary greatly in how they treat different items of property and in what dollar limits they place on each class of property. However, in most states you increase your likelihood of losing property if you have assets such as vehicles and homes that are almost paid off.

People who live in states with low zones of protection have the option of filing a Chapter 13 bankruptcy. They will have to pay out in the Chapter 13 at least at least as much as the creditors would have received in a Chapter 7, but they have several years to do so.

Section 8

ALTERNATIVES TO BANKRUPTCY

- How do people respond when they have money problems?
- Why should I be careful in trying debt consolidation once I already have money problems?
- What are some of the disadvantages to borrowing against my home?
- Isn't it better to borrow against my retirement fund than to file bankruptcy?
- Can I get a bill consolidation loan?
- Why is it so hard to negotiate with creditors?
- Can Consumer Credit Counseling help?
- Can a debt consolidation agency help?

How do people respond when they have money problems?

Most people go through four different stages as they face financial hard times and before they consider filing for bankruptcy.

1. They try to lower their expenses or borrow additional funds to tide them over.
2. They attempt to deal with collection efforts by explaining their situation to the creditors and collectors and try to work with the creditors to arrange lower payments.
3. They consider a credit service that will attempt to work with their creditors for them.
4. They talk with a bankruptcy lawyer.

This is a logical sequence of responses, but people often tend to rush through some stages and spend too much time in others.

Stage 1 is a particular problem for people. They try to trim expenses, often without drawing up detailed budgets for their accounts. This is a huge mistake. The importance of budgets cannot be overstated. Income will vary from month to month, but this should not preclude making a budget for expenses. Expenses also vary from month to month with taxes, insurance, and heat being higher in some months than others. By going over several months' or years' bills, you can develop a monthly average. This will form the basis for your future decisions and calculations. Section 4 has some typical household categories that you can use as a template for developing your budget.

With a budget set out, you can make decisions on where to cut spending. On the personal side, you will find that there are only a few places you can cut. Food, clothing, and entertainment are typically the most viable options. Items like house and car payments, on the other hand, are fixed and are missed only at the risk of causing severe problems.

> **Note:** If you are to the point where you are skipping house or car payments or are not paying taxes, you have severe problems and are likely beyond making simple expense adjustments.

Why should I be careful in trying debt consolidation once I already have money problems?

We often meet with people who have lost their homes or are four to eight months behind on their house payments. When asked how they got so far behind, many tell the same story—they were working on getting a refinancing loan on their house and the loan never came through, or when it came through, it was much more expensive than they had been told. Often people aren't shown the terms of these ugly loans—with high interest rates and closing fees—until they go to close. At that time they have no choice but to accept, regardless of terms; they are months behind on their original loan and the creditors want all of their money in one lump payment right away. The signee must either take the new high cost loan or lose their house.

These people have been the victims of unscrupulous loan brokers. There is a great deal of money to be made by matching up a lender and a borrower. Of course, this money can only be made if a borrower will wait around while the broker tries different lenders. Sometimes a match is made right away; sometimes it takes a long time. If it does take a long time, it is very important to the broker to keep the borrower available. Some unscrupulous brokers get business by promising everyone who calls that there is a very good chance they will get the loan. This gets the borrower tied in with them. Then they tell all types of stories about missing papers, people out sick, etc., to keep the borrower from trying anything else.

Before you borrow against your home, keep these simple facts in mind.

1. Do not borrow against your home to pay off credit cards or other unsecured debts. Most people do not solve their debt problems by doing this. After all, their house payments go up and they are exchanging debt that a lawyer or Consumer Credit Counseling can do something about for a house mortgage that no one can do anything about. *You must pay every cent on time or you will lose your house.*

2. It normally takes about a week or two after you provide your information to know whether or not your loan is approved. Never wait for more than thirty days to find out about a loan. If you've been waiting longer than that, see a lawyer or Consumer Credit Counseling at once.

3. Do not pay any attention to how nice brokers are. They are always nice. The real test is whether or not they get you the loan in a reasonable period of time. If not, see a lawyer or Consumer Credit Counseling about your money problems.

Note: If your house is being foreclosed on, see an attorney at once. You do not have time to get—and probably cannot afford—a refinance loan. Do not pay any attention to a loan broker who tells you not to worry about the foreclosure. The loan broker may not be able to take care of the problem. Too many people have lost their homes while waiting for someone who told him or her not to worry. It does not matter to a broker if you lose your house, but he or she may make money off of you if you stick around during delays in your processing.

What are some of the disadvantages to borrowing against my home?

As we mentioned in Section 6, it is a high-risk gamble to borrow against your home to pay off other debts. It sounds so logical. Replace your many high interest rate credit card payments with one low, tax-deductible payment.

Keep in mind what you are doing.

- You are making a bet. If you lose the bet you lose your home. The bet is that you will not have any more credit card debt after you refinance your house. Many of the people who refinance to pay off credit cards again charge on their cards. Now they have two debts, a big house payment and credit card payments on top of that.

- You are betting nothing bad will happen to you. You assume you will not have a drop in income, you or your family will not get sick (and miss work), or you will not have big medical bills. You assume you and your mate will not split up or that you will not have to take on the care of a parent, a child, or a grandchild. If one of these happens and you are maxed out on your home debt because of refinancing, then you are in danger of losing your home.

- You have exchanged a debt that would have been paid off in the short term by making maximum payments for one you are likely to be paying for twenty-five or thirty years.

- You have exchanged a debt that a bankruptcy lawyer or Consumer Credit Counseling can do something about for one that cannot be modified.

Isn't it better to borrow against my retirement fund than to file bankruptcy?

Another thing many people do when they have financial problems is borrow against their retirement money. As we discussed elsewhere, this is a terrible idea.

Something can be done about most debts, even houses that are being foreclosed on, but once your retirement money is gone, it is gone. Social Security will not be enough to retire on. If you spend your retirement money, you will not be able to retire, and you will have to work when you are older. There are not many jobs actively recruiting older people. This is why one sees so many senior citizens supplementing their incomes with jobs that teenagers used to do, such as bagging groceries and working at fast food restaurants. You may think your children will help you, but your kids will likely have problems of their own.

Hold on to your retirement money. Before you even think about taking money out of your retirement account because of financial problems, see a bankruptcy lawyer or Consumer Credit Counseling.

Can I get a bill consolidation loan?

Many people feel that if they could just get a debt consolidation loan they could come through their financial crisis. The idea of exchanging many payments for one is seductive. Unfortunately, this is seldom the answer to one's financial problems.

Financial institutions are reluctant to loan money to people who are having financial problems because of a drop in income. They will look at a potential borrower's cash flow to see if the monthly loan payment can be made. Far too often there is little or no income to make the loan payments.

They will also look at the potential borrower's *debt to income ratio* (a number computed by dividing your income by your debt). If you already have high debts, a lender is unlikely to give you money so that you can pay off other lenders.

Even if you can obtain a debt consolidation loan while you are experiencing a financial crisis, you are likely to be charged a high interest rate. This will make paying off a new loan harder, and it will take longer. In addition, the high interest rate will mean your total monthly payments on the one loan are unlikely to be smaller than the sum of your other loans.

Why is it so hard to negotiate with creditors?

As noted in Section 3, dealing with creditors can be one of the worst experiences of your life. They are frequently rude, threatening, and abusive. When harassed, most people with debts attempt to explain why they are unable to pay their bills and arrange to make partial payments for a while. This is a waste of time and emotional energy.

The collection process typically relies on teams of collectors working accounts. You may have a long conversation with "Joe" and work something out, and two days later "Sue" will call and deny any knowledge of this arrangement, insult you, and demand payment in full.

Even if you are only dealing with one creditor, your sincere efforts to explain yourself are not likely to work. Even the most kind-hearted collection agents become hardened after a while. They are lied to often and hear false promises from many debtors. In addition, the collection process demands results, and the system seems to have concluded that being rude and unreasonable is more cost-effective than being understanding and taking reduced payments. Thus you may be able, through great effort, to work out something with a few creditors, but the odds of getting all of your creditors to work with you are low.

Can Consumer Credit Counseling help?

Consumer Credit Counseling (CCC) is a non-profit organization, often affiliated with The United Way, which is supported in part by the credit industry. Typically, you go into their offices and meet face to face with a counselor. The charge to you is very low, as much of the financial support for CCC comes from the credit industry and The United Way. The value is high because the counselor, at your individual session, will go over your budget and analyze your debt status.

One great value of CCC is they will help you look at your personal budget and see what can be changed. CCC will normally set you up on a repayment plan that lasts about three to five years, and you will pay back all of the debt plus interest. Often a notation that you were in a CCC program will go on your credit report, but this is probably less damaging to your credit than many late payments, foreclosures, repossessions, or bankruptcy.

Can a debt consolidation agency help?

There are a growing number of other third-party intermediaries. You've likely seen their ads on TV. They go by the names of debt counselors or debt consolidation agencies and are typically labeled in their ads as nonprofit companies. Keep in mind that the term *nonprofit* does not mean the company doesn't make money. They often make very good money, and their employees can earn a high salary. The term means that no profits are paid out—it is all spent on operating costs and salaries—or that there are no shareholders who are entitled to profits. These companies typically make their money by charging you a handling fee or by reaching an agreement with the creditor to let them have part of the money collected in exchange for collecting monthly payments from you and sending the money to the creditor.

Debt consolidators say they will work out a deal with your creditors where you make one payment to the consolidator and they in turn pay your creditors. Unlike lawyers or the credit bureau, many of these operators are not licensed or regulated, so there are no limits on what they can do. A few merely take your money and do not send it to anyone, so after months of faithfully making payments, you are out of money and still have the debt in full. Many are able to make arrangements with a portion, but not all, of your creditors. This means that the remaining creditors will still be calling you. Other consolidators may take your money and then, keeping a cut for themselves, make the minimum payment to your creditors. At the rate they make payments for you, it could be many years before your debts are paid off.

> **Note:** Be very careful of anyone who does not have a local office you can go to. Visit their office before you send them any of your money. Find out if they are regulated by your state or are a United Way agency. If not, be careful of dealing with them.

If you use such a service, you should track what is happening to your loans very carefully. All too often people think things are going fine. They are making their monthly payments and the phone calls from creditors have largely stopped. It is only after several months that they learn their loan balances have not gone down. Ask specifically how long the payments will take to settle or pay off your debt, because they are charging you each month and the organization may have an incentive to keep you in the plan as long as possible.

You should also know that several states have moved to close down businesses operating as nonprofit credit services.

MYTHS ABOUT DEBT AND BANKRUPTCY

- What are the most common myths about bankruptcy?
- Will bankruptcy ruin my credit?
- Will notice of my bankruptcy be put into the newspaper or become public?
- Will bankruptcy ruin my spouse's credit?
- Will I lose my home and cars?
- Will I lose all my other property because of the bankruptcy?
- Will the bankruptcy people sell my property at an auction in front of my home?
- If I file bankruptcy, does my spouse have to file too?
- Will my spouse and I lose our jobs if we file bankruptcy?
- Will I lose my license?
- Will I be able to get student loans?
- Can I have a bank account?
- Will I be put in jail if I do not pay my bills?
- Will my debts go away in time if I just ignore them?
- If I declare bankruptcy, does that mean I can never have credit again?

What are the most common myths about bankruptcy?

When people consider bankruptcy, they experience all sorts of vague fears based on snippets of information they have heard over the years, advice from well-meaning friends and family, and their own rising fears and concerns.

The most common concerns—each discussed in this section—are:

- It will ruin my credit.
- Notice of my bankruptcy will be put in the newspaper or become public.
- It will ruin my spouse's credit.
- I will lose my house and cars.
- I will lose my other property.
- They will sell my property at auction in front of my home.
- If I file bankruptcy, my spouse will have to file also.
- My spouse and I will lose our jobs.
- I will lose my license.
- I won't be able to get student loans.
- I can no longer have a bank account.
- I will be put in jail if I do not pay my bills.
- The debts will just go away in time if I ignore them.
- I can never have good credit again.

Will bankruptcy ruin my credit?

It is not uncommon for people considering bankruptcy to have very good credit. Over the years they have been careful to pay their bills on time and as a consequence have been able to borrow large sums of money. Then something happens—loss of income, illness, injury, or divorce. Because of one or more of these life events, they begin to have trouble paying their bills on time. Often people will hold off financial problems by dipping into their savings and selling off assets. But the day comes when they do not have the funds to make their monthly payments for debts.

Normally people hold on, hoping for the tide to turn as collection calls from creditors increase in volume and harshness. In most cases it is only then that people begin to think about bankruptcy and see a lawyer.

Reading about bankruptcy or seeing a lawyer is a symptom of financial problems. If one concludes bankruptcy is the only way to address one's financial problems, it is not the bankruptcy that is going to ruin one's credit. The person's credit status is already in trouble. To put it in medical terms, a fever is not what makes you sick—the fever is a symptom of an underlying bodily illness or injury. Bankruptcy is the financial fever and is the symptom of the underlying financial problem. A bankruptcy notation on your credit report is a strong negative, but so are car repossessions, home fore-closures, many slow pays, and a high debt load. The key is to see if you are any worse off with a bankruptcy.

Will notice of my bankruptcy be put into the newspaper or become public?

People are embarrassed when they face financial problems. It is often viewed as a prime capitalist sin. They want their financial affairs to be strictly private. For this reason, they often worry that the fact they filed for bankruptcy will be put into the paper. They have vague memories of reading about bankruptcy filings, but they were busy and did not really read the story.

Rest assured, there is almost no chance your personal bankruptcy will end up in the newspaper. Stories about bankruptcy focus on large companies with many employees and suppliers—the type of thing that will interest a broad readership. Your personal bankruptcy filing is of limited interest to readers and not worth the limited space a newspaper has in its daily or weekly edition.

However, one cannot entirely rule out the possibility that the news would be put in the paper. Some small local papers are very hard up for items to put in the paper and, in theory, could choose to print the filing of your bankruptcy. Bankruptcy filings are public records, and anyone can go to the bankruptcy courthouse and look up bankruptcy filings or even do so online if they know how. However, even then the odds are very low. Bankruptcy courts cover a very large population base, and many counties are under the jurisdiction of the court. This means a very large number of filings will have to be searched to locate the ones that would have any possible significance to the few readers of the small local paper. This is not a good use of the newspaper's limited resources.

Another factor protecting your privacy is that most newspapers view this type of personal problem as beyond the scope of what a newspaper should cover. They are not gossip sheets or purveyors of personal problems.

We must reiterate, however, that bankruptcies are matters of public record. That means there will be a file at the bankruptcy courthouse that can be examined by any member of the public. The same is true of the records of most lawsuits at the county courthouse. But accessing these records is not easy. They are not set up for someone to just thumb through; they must have your specific name to pull your file. This makes it very unlikely a friend or neighbor will just stumble on your file. And of course, there is the time and effort involved in physically going to the courthouse— something almost no one is willing to take the trouble to do.

The courts have set bankruptcy records on the Internet. This removes one barrier of finding out about bankruptcy—the physical effort. The records can be reached from a home or business.

However, this search is not very easy. The layout of the web page is government-designed and is not made for ease of use. It takes a great deal more effort to navigate the website than most people are willing to undertake. It is not designed for browsing. You must have a specific name or case number to pull up a file. This makes it unlikely that anyone will, by accident, stumble upon the fact that you filed bankruptcy.

Some businesses systematically go through bankruptcy filings for their own commercial purposes. The credit bureau does this. Some banks or groups of banks collect this information. Credit card companies, lenders, and mortgage brokers also systematically search the bankruptcy records. Their purpose is to make offers to you for credit cards or new car loans. Thus, to sum up, as far as publishing the filing of your bankruptcy, the most likely result will be to put you on additional mailing lists for credit cards and loans.

Will bankruptcy ruin my spouse's credit?

People are naturally worried about their spouse or future spouses. They say things like, "My wife had nothing to do with my debts—I don't want her credit hurt," or, "I'm about to get married. Will the bankruptcy affect my new husband's credit?"

Barring a mistake on the part of the credit bureau or a creditor, spouses are not affected if one member of a marriage files or has filed bankruptcy. Each person has a separate file at the credit bureau and is tracked by their social security number. Thus, assuming the spouse is not a codebtor, wiping out a debt in bankruptcy by one member of a marriage should not affect the credit of the spouse.

Some creditors will try to tell your spouse that they must pay this debt, because they are married to the debtor. This is only a collection tactic that takes advantage of people's lack of knowledge about the law.

Occasionally a debt or bankruptcy will show up on a spouse's credit report. This is almost always removed when the spouse objects to the entry because there is no legal basis for such a claim. Of course, if the spouse is a codebtor, then the debt and the bankruptcy will affect the spouse. Each codebtor is responsible for all of the debt, and if one does not pay, the creditors can take collection efforts against the other codebtor.

Will I lose my home and cars?

This is a realistic possibility depending on what state you reside in. Most states allow people who file bankruptcy to retain a home and a car up to a certain value. The value of homes will range from unlimited value in Texas and Florida, to very little in other states. Most states range from $5,000 to $30,000. This is free equity in the home, so the amount of the mortgage(s) must be deducted from the market value to obtain the free value of the house. Clearly, if you own your home free of all debt, you will (in most states) lose it in bankruptcy. But most people trying to keep afloat have borrowed against their homes before they consider bankruptcy, so their free equity in the home is limited.

> **Note:** Federal and state exemptions are set up to protect people's main residence, so vacation homes and rental property cannot claim exemption.

Cars work the same way. Most states allow you to keep one vehicle. Most states allow between $1,000 and $5,000 in free value for your vehicle. It is not uncommon to see people at the end of their financial rope who still own cars and trucks free and clear. These people will be faced with the prospect of giving up their vehicles or borrowing money from family members to pay the trustee the difference between the exemption amount and the value of the vehicle.

> **Note:** Protection is normally offered to one vehicle per person, so if you own several cars—including cars used by your children—you stand to lose those extra cars, unless there are loans against them for more than their value.

Will I lose all my other property because of the bankruptcy?

This is a constant fear of those in debt. Much of what the bankruptcy lawyer does is define what property could possibly be taken by the bankruptcy court system and what could not. Most people who file bankruptcy will lose very little of their property, as every state allows a bankruptcy filer to keep a certain amount of personal property (furniture, clothes, appliances, etc.) with which to get a fresh start. The great majority of our filers lose nothing.

However, there are exceptions. These normally come when the filer has more property than the average person—an expensive house filled with fine furniture, several vehicles that are paid for, vacation or rental houses, collections that have a ready market, antiques, silver collections, expensive paintings, etc. What states allow people to keep is fairly bare-boned; extras and expensive luxuries are likely to be taken by the bankruptcy system.

Will the bankruptcy people sell my property at an auction in front of my home?

The idea of not only losing one's property, but having it sold in a public way in front of one's neighbors, is horrifying. This almost never happens. The idea seems to come from seeing auctions of farm equipment as part of the TV news. Accounts of farmers' bankruptcies and the sale of their equipment are sometimes put on the air as news stories. These sales often happen at the farm. A farm is a business and the farm equipment and livestock have a high value and are hard to physically move. It makes economic sense to hold a sale where these items are located. The same is true of a store's inventory—although these sales often owe more to marketing hype than the bankruptcy process.

We have never seen a case where the trustee had household goods of such value that he or she would dream of having a sale at a person's house. It is far more effective to hold a sale of personal property at a central sales location where buyers are used to coming to purchase items. Because the great majority of personal property is never taken and sold, there would be no sale in the first place.

It is possible, but unlikely, to have a home sold at public auction. This happens when a person files for bankruptcy, gives up his or her home, and the mortgages against it are so low that there will be something for the trustee to recover if he or she has an auction of the home. In such a case, the trustee is likely to put ads in the newspaper saying a house at a given address will be sold at auction as part of the bankruptcy of "John Doe." The reason this does not happen in most cases is that people are careful to not file bankruptcy if they will run the risk of having their home taken from them by the trustee.

If I file bankruptcy, does my spouse have to file too?

People often worry about dragging their spouse into bankruptcy. They think that if one member of the marriage files, the other must also file. This is not correct. Bankruptcy is an individual process, and one spouse files without the other all the time. However, spouses often find it makes sense to file together as both owe money to the same creditors. To have just one file in such a case would merely throw the debts back on the other.

In many cases, both spouses are not liable for the debts. One spouse may have taken out all the loans and credit cards. Or one of the spouses may have incurred the debts before the marriage, so the debts are only in that person's name. In such cases, one individual filing makes sense and is desirable. Having only one spouse file leaves the other spouse without debt and without a bankruptcy on his or her credit history.

But remember, while the debts are often only in one spouse's name, many of their assets are in both names. Make a careful examination of property owned and its value before a spouse files bankruptcy alone, just as you would if you filed jointly. Also, keep in mind that the nonfiling spouse's income must be counted—subject to his or her own offsets—in working out the filer's means test.

Will my spouse and I lose our jobs if we file bankruptcy?

People do not automatically lose their jobs if they file bankruptcy and their employer learns of it. In fact, it is illegal to terminate someone because he or she filed for bankruptcy. Many employers never know that you filed for bankruptcy. Those who do know will often be glad you have addressed the financial problems that were bothering you and causing you to receive collection phone calls at work. In addition, the employer may feel safer. Sometimes people embezzle money from employers in an effort to pay their debts. This temptation is gone if your debts have been addressed in bankruptcy.

It must be said, however, that there are some employers who do not look with favor on a bankruptcy filing. Normally, these are employers in the financial industry, who lose money because of bankruptcy. Others are in the business of handling customers' money and feel it does not look good if one of their employees lets their personal finances get away from them. The bankruptcy system will almost always work with you so that you can protect your job if you have this type of employer.

Will I lose my license?

The government regulates many activities. It issues drivers' licenses and licenses to engage in certain professions—barbers, insurance sales, doctors, contractors, and stockbrokers. Some businesses involve licenses to handle other people's money—insurance sales, financial managers, and stockbrokers. The majority of these people have not lost their licenses because of filing for bankruptcy, and many have even obtained licenses in some of these fields after bankruptcy. However, a blanket statement cannot be made, as these licenses are normally issued by the individual state and local governments. These rules can vary greatly from one local area to another. Many of these rules may require disclosure of a bankruptcy filing. Just to be safe, it is a good idea to ask about the licensing agency's policies before you file for bankruptcy.

Will I be able to get student loans?

College and graduate school are very important. People often worry that they or their children will not be able to obtain student loans if they file bankruptcy. This fear is overblown. Loans for college and graduate school come from two sources. One is a government-guaranteed student loan pool, and the other is regular borrowing from a bank that is to be used to pay for schooling. Eligibility for government-guaranteed student loans—the great majority of loans used for schooling—is not affected by a bankruptcy.

Borrowing from banks based solely on your credit is another matter. These loans, like any other loan, will be affected for several years until you rebuild your credit.

Can I have a bank account?

A person who is in bankruptcy or who has filed bankruptcy in the past is not prevented by law from having a checking or savings account with a bank or other financial institution.

If you have a bank account with a bank you owe money to, it is often advisable to close that bank account or keep an amount of no more than a few dollars in it. This is because the banks that have money owed to them can freeze your account and collect the money to pay off the debts owed to them. This is called the right of offset. It means if I hold money for you, and you owe me money because of a debt, I can dip into the money I hold for you to satisfy the debt. For this reason people going through bankruptcy often close their bank accounts at the bank or credit union they have been doing business with.

Some people may find it difficult to open an account with a new bank after filing for bankruptcy. Banks do not have to do business with you, and some choose not to deal with people who have filed bankruptcy. However, banking is a competitive business, and there is no shortage of institutions willing to deal with you after your filing—you just have to search a little harder and perhaps go to a bank location that is less convenient.

Will I be put in jail if I do not pay my bills?

Fear of jail or arrest because a bill is not paid is not unusual among people who owe money. Bill collectors often play on this fear by threatening that they will send the sheriff out to see the debtor if the bill is not paid. Rest assured that no one is ever put in jail for simply owing money. This might have happened hundreds of years ago, but not in the modern United States. Debt is what is called a *civil matter*—it is between two people or businesses and does not involve the government. It is not a breach of law (such as murder or robbery), which means you cannot be put in jail.

Will my debts go away in time if I just ignore them?

If you cannot be jailed for debt, why file bankruptcy at all? Debts show up on your credit report for only seven years and you do not own anything of value—why even consider bankruptcy? If you own little property, you are what lawyers call judgment proof. That is, a judgment can be taken against you, but there is nothing to collect. Some states allow wage garnishments to collect on a private civil debt, but some do not. This being the case—particularly if you live in a non-garnishment state or have irregular income—why worry about the debt?

Just because the debt is removed from your credit report does not mean you no longer owe the creditor. The obligation to pay a debt can easily last longer than seven years. If you ignore the creditors' claims, they can obtain a judgment against you. Now this becomes an enduring legal matter.

The judgment becomes a judgment lien. If you should acquire a home or land in the locale where the judgment is docketed, the judgment can attach itself against your real property. When you go to transfer the property, the buyer will normally require that the judgment plus interest be paid. In this way, the debt and judgment limit your ability to get back on your feet and move ahead. Judgment liens do not go away for a long time, and in fact, if your land or home becomes more valuable, the creditor may be allowed to seize the property.

As if that weren't enough, a creditor obtaining a judgment starts the seven-year credit report clock running again. The applicable time period on your credit report is not just seven years from the original debt, but seven years from the last major activity on the debt.

If I declare bankruptcy, does that mean I can never have credit again?

Simply put, no. It may take some time and effort on your part, but you can have access to credit again. Section 18 covers this in more detail.

Section 10

OVERVIEW OF BANKRUPTCY AND HOW IT WORKS

- What are the different types of bankruptcy?
- What is a Chapter 7 bankruptcy?
- What is a Chapter 11 bankruptcy?
- What is a Chapter 12 bankruptcy?
- What is a Chapter 13 bankruptcy?
- Is it possible to owe too much money to file bankruptcy?
- How do the different types of bankruptcies compare to each other?

What are the different types of bankruptcy?

People speak generally of bankruptcy without realizing that there are several types of bankruptcy that operate quite differently. An individual or a corporation can apply for a Chapter 7 or Chapter 11 bankruptcy. Only an individual can apply for a Chapter 13 bankruptcy. In bankruptcy, an individual can *exempt* (protect) certain property necessary to live—normally shelter, personal property, and transportation. These exemptions, however, can only offer limited protection. See Appendix A for state specific information.

What is a Chapter 7 bankruptcy?

Chapter 7 bankruptcy is the type of bankruptcy most people think about when they speak of bankruptcy. It can be filed by either an individual or a corporation. It will wipe out many debts in their entirety. Thus, if you owe $40,000 on credit cards and medical bills, a Chapter 7 bankruptcy would completely eliminate these debts. Some debts—such as certain taxes, secured loans, student loans, and child support—are not wiped out. You must continue to make payments on your home if you wish to keep it, and you will generally need to pay money for any back taxes you owe or make arrangements with the taxing authority.

The trade-off for the clean, relatively debt-free, fresh start of a Chapter 7 bankruptcy is that some of your personal and business assets might be taken and sold by the court to partially fulfill your debt. The money from the sale of your assets is distributed to your creditors. However, there are exceptions to this rule that in many cases will keep you from losing most your property.

Each person who files a Chapter 7 bankruptcy will—depending on what state he or she lives in—have a list of the property and dollar limits he or she can keep despite filing for bankruptcy. In most cases this will mean that the debtor keeps his or her home, furniture, cars, and personal property. Of course, because these items are often *security* (collateral) for debt, the property must still be paid for in monthly installments as was originally contracted, as *secured goods*.

What is a Chapter 11 bankruptcy?

Chapter 11 bankruptcies often get front-page headlines in the news. They affect workers, suppliers, and other creditors. Though in some ways more infamous than a Chapter 7, this is actually a better solution for workers and creditors as it keeps the business alive, preserves at least some jobs, and pays back some debt.

An individual, as well as a business, can file a Chapter 11 bankruptcy. However, for reasons we shall discuss, a Chapter 11 bankruptcy is often not suitable for an individual, even if that person runs a business.

First, the same basic steps must be followed and reported completely regardless of whether you own a huge, national company or a small, single-store operation, which makes a Chapter 11 bankruptcy quite expensive.

The second problem is that the underlying purpose of a Chapter 11 bankruptcy is to give time to renegotiate fixed contracts and dispose of unprofitable assets in an orderly way. If you are a person selling your skills—a painter or a lawyer, for example—there are unlikely to be fixed contracts to renegotiate or unprofitable assets to give away. If you have only one store location that is not generating sufficient sales to cover your expenses or earn a profit, the problem is your core business, not your contracts or extra locations.

In a Chapter 11 bankruptcy, a business owner files for bankruptcy to stop collection efforts by creditors. The business continues to operate under the direction of the court. Often, the management of the business stays in place and runs the business while the details of the bankruptcy are worked out.

When a Chapter 11 bankruptcy is filed, the lawyers of the creditors often come into court to try to protect their clients' interests, and you must often pay your own lawyer large sums of money to fight your creditors' lawyers. Because the court has taken control of your business assets, this requires you to file special periodic reports explaining the ongoing financial health of your business and what the managers are doing. This often requires special accountants and always takes a great deal of your manager's time. Normally, a bankruptcy lawyer will require a very large payment up front before he or she undertakes to file for Chapter 11 bankruptcy because of the system's complexity, the stringent drafting requirements, and the many trips to court.

The whole process is designed to establish a plan of reorganization. The *plan of reorganization* will detail how each group or *class* of creditors is to be treated and who will receive what. Each class of creditors then votes on the plan. The plan is approved only if it meets a number of complex rules, which are beyond the scope of this short overview. The plan must receive the approval of a certain number of the classes. This is very different from a Chapter 7 bankruptcy where approval of the creditors is not required.

Of course, no lawyer would draw up a plan and present it for a vote without finding out how key members of the different groups are likely to vote. There is often a great deal of talking among the lawyers for the bankruptcy filer and the different creditors, all of which costs money. The need for a team of accountants, lawyers, and managers to deal with the bankruptcy issues does not matter all that much to a *Fortune* 500 company but will swamp a small business. For this reason individuals seldom file a Chapter 11 bankruptcy, and those who do, often end up converting to a Chapter 7 bankruptcy.

What is a Chapter 12 bankruptcy?

Congress has enacted the *Chapter 12 bankruptcy* provisions to meet the special problems faced by farmers. A farmer has expenses every month, but the income from the sale of animals, fruits, and grains typically comes only once or twice a year. The Chapter 12 bankruptcy is a specialized form of business bankruptcy to meet this unusual money flow problem.

What is a Chapter 13 bankruptcy?

Chapter 13 bankruptcy is often called a wage-earner plan or a debt-consolidation plan. It was originally set up for people who have a steady regular income and who could, if given time, pay at least a portion of their debts. Gradually, the protection of a Chapter 13 bankruptcy was expanded to include people who did not have a steady income—for example, salespeople and waitstaff.

In a Chapter 13 bankruptcy, the debtor discloses his or her income and sets up a plan for paying creditors over a three- to five-year period. The debtor is not as likely to have assets at risk of being taken, like he or she would under a Chapter 7 bankruptcy, because money is being paid to the creditors. The steady monthly payments—often made through an automatic wage deduction—that the debtor makes to the Chapter 13 trustee is distributed to the different creditors in accordance with a plan of repayment that the debtor filed with the bankruptcy court. In these ways, a Chapter 13 bankruptcy is a lot like a Chapter 11 bankruptcy.

Is it possible to owe too much money to file bankruptcy?

It is possible to owe too much money to file a Chapter 13 bankruptcy. Only an individual with noncontingent liquidated unsecured debts of less than $336,900 and noncontingent liquidated secured debts of less than $1,010,650 can file a Chapter 13 bankruptcy.

These dollar amounts will change each year. Normally, they will increase with inflation. However, there is no cap on how much you owe to file a Chapter 7 if you are an individual or a corporation.

How do the different types of bankruptcies compare to each other?

The main difference between a Chapter 11 bankruptcy and a Chapter 13 bankruptcy is one of scale and oversight. Because a Chapter 13 bankruptcy deals with smaller dollar amounts and so many of them are filed, there is less oversight by the court and often less involvement of the creditors.

In the regulatory system set up by Congress, there are provisions for continuing to operate large businesses (Chapter 11), farms (Chapter 12), and for individual workers (Chapter 13), but there is nothing designed for the special problem of small business owners. This means that a small business entrepreneur who wants to keep on running a business must try to fit into the provisions of a Chapter 13 bankruptcy or a Chapter 11 bankruptcy, or file a Chapter 7 bankruptcy and start over. Which type of bankruptcy a small business owner files depends on his or her goals. If he or she is willing to give up personal and business assets, he or she would choose a Chapter 7. If the small business owner wishes to keep running the business, his or her only options are Chapter 11 or Chapter 13. Chapter 11 bankruptcy is not a realistic option for most small business owners. This leaves a Chapter 13 bankruptcy—the wage earner's plan.

Section 11

CONSUMER BANKRUPTCY CONCEPTS

- What is median family income and why is it important?
- What is current monthly income?
- What is an IRS budget?
- What is the means test?
- How are vehicle values determined in bankruptcy?
- What is credit counseling?
- What are reaffirmation agreements?
- What happens if I move to another state before I file bankruptcy?

What is median family income and why is it important?

When the Bankruptcy Code was changed in 2005, the concept of *median family income* was introduced. This is an income point at which half the families of a given size will earn more than that income, and half will earn less. There is a different median income for each family size—one member, two members, etc. In addition, median incomes are computed by state, so the median income for a family of three in Ohio will likely be different from that of a family of three in New York. Median family income is computed using gross income.

Median family income is determined in each case using both spouses' income, whether one or both spouses are filing for bankruptcy. If the filer is above the state's median family income, he or she will have to pass a means test or will be forced to file a Chapter 13. Whether or not this happens will be determined by further calculations using an IRS budget and the means test (see below).

What is current monthly income?

To see if a given family, which can be only one person, is above the state's median income, one must establish the family's *current monthly income*. This is a term of art and includes income from the last six months. Income from almost all sources, whether or not taxable, is counted.

The one major exception is for payments that are not received regularly; a one-time gift of $1,000 from your mother need not be counted, but monthly gifts of $50 from her must be counted as income. Also, Social Security payments are not counted, but military pensions are. Payments received as victims of war crimes or victims of international or domestic terrorism are not counted. The sum of all the payments that are counted over the last six months are divided by 6 to come up with current monthly income.

If a married debtor plans to file alone, the income of both husband and wife still must be counted. There are special provisions to cover cases where the parties are separated and rules to determine whether the parties are really separated.

What is an IRS budget?

Prior to the 2005 changes to the bankruptcy laws, defining reasonable living expenses for a debtor was up to the judge. For debtors who are above their state's median income this discussion, in theory, is largely removed. The bankruptcy laws order that these debtors will, for the most part, live on a budget determined by the IRS in dealing with collection cases.

Depending on where you live, the IRS budget can be reasonable or very tight, as most of its categories are set on a national or regional level. Examples are food, health care, clothing, and other household items. Home ownership costs and rental costs are set by family size and by county of a given state. Vehicle ownership and operational costs are set by region.

What is the means test?

The means test is a mathematical calculation working out if the filing debtor has enough money left over to pay a Chapter 13 plan. The means test starts with the debtor's current monthly income. The formula takes away the proper IRS living expenses, alimony, child support, and projected Chapter 13 administrative expenses—health insurance, disability insurance, etc. Reasonable charitable contributions are allowed as deductions. The debtor can also deduct expenses. Reasonably necessary expenses incurred to maintain safety from family violence or for the care and support of an elderly, chronically ill, or disabled household member or member of the debtor's immediate family who cannot pay these expenses themselves. Withholding taxes are deducted.

If a debtor is filing without his or her spouse, that spouse's separate expenses, (e.g., vehicle payments, child support, credit card payments) are taken away because the spouse's income was counted as part of the debtor's household monthly income.

Next, payments on secured items such as houses, vehicles, stoves, etc. are taken away and other technical adjustments are made.

The resulting number is what the debtor in theory could pay to the court for the benefit of his or her creditors each month. There is a several-pronged test to see if the debtor has enough money left over to make a Chapter 13 worth the bankruptcy system's effort. This involves seeing if the debtor's monthly income, after the above deductions, and multiplied by 60 is not less than the lesser of:

- 25% of the debtor's non-priority unsecured debts in the case, or $6,575, whichever is greater; or,
- $10,950.

This is the amount of money that would go to unsecured creditors. The actual plan payment would be higher as it would include administrative fees, and likely payments on secured items such as vehicles, appliances, and other secured items. If the debtor's gross family income was above his or her state's median income for their family size, he or she will be forced to a five-year Chapter 13 plan.

If a debtor and his or her lawyer tries to file a Chapter 7 when the means test shows he or she could file a Chapter 13, the filing is classed as an abusive filing, and the debtor is forced into a Chapter 13.

The combination of the complex nature of the means test and the possibility of punishment if an error is made by the lawyer in computing it to see which chapter bankruptcy a debtor should be in has caused many lawyers to stop doing bankruptcy work.

How are vehicle values determined in bankruptcy?

Most people feel they have a good idea of the value of their vehicle. They are surprised when the bankruptcy system places a higher value on it.

Generally speaking, the system values the vehicle at what the debtor would have to pay to purchase that vehicle at retail from a dealer in the condition it is in now. What the debtor could sell the vehicle for is of no importance.

This value is obtained from a Kelly Blue Book or NADA Book, depending on the local court. In many, but not all courts, the full retail price may be adjusted down to take account of dealer preparation costs. So, the value of the vehicle may be 95% or 90% or even 70% of the full retail price.

For purposes of finding your equity in the vehicle, subtract the amount owed on the vehicle from the court-determined value. This gives you the vehicle value you use in working with state exemptions.

What is credit counseling?

There are two types of credit counseling. The first is to obtain a fix on where you stand financially and what options you have. This is done by general counseling services. You can find a list of contacts for such general counseling services organized by state in Appendix B.

The second type of counseling is required to file a bankruptcy petition. When the bankruptcy code was amended in 2005, an additional step was added. Each debtor who plans to file a bankruptcy must first undergo credit counseling.

The people and organizations doing the counseling must be approved by the local bankruptcy system—usually the administrator in each bankruptcy district. Normally, they will keep a list of who they have approved to be counselors.

You must complete credit counseling. If a case is filed without a certificate that credit counseling has taken place, the case will be dismissed. There is no way to fix this error. There are provisions for emergency situations, but the courts do not tend to be very sympathetic. One of the reasons for the court's hard line is that in many cases credit counseling can be done via computer, so there is no problem getting appointments.

The original purpose of credit counseling was to make sure that people with money problems understood all their options before they filed for bankruptcy. But, the assumption that this was needed has not been born out in practice. In the real world, people are very careful before they file bankruptcy and have thought their options through. So the credit counseling step, rather than being a help, in most cases turns out to be an extra expense on the way to filing a bankruptcy.

There is one twist to the pre-petition credit counseling requirement. In most districts it cannot take place on the same day the bankruptcy petition is filed. The reasoning seems to be that the credit counseling is supposed to give you options besides filing bankruptcy and you need at least one day to think about those options.

What are reaffirmation agreements?

In a *reaffirmation agreement*, a creditor and a debtor, who could discharge a debt, agree that the debt will be paid.

The bankruptcy code is very detailed in how these reaffirmations are to be done. A detailed disclosure form must be filled out and signed by the debtor. It is then filed with the court for the court's review.

The debtor's lawyer is to sign the affidavit that:

1. the agreement does not impose an undue hardship on the debtor or his or her dependents;
2. it represents a fully informed and voluntary agreement by the debtor; and,
3. the lawyer has fully advised the debtor of the legal effect and consequences of the agreement and any default.

There may be times when the debtor is not represented by a lawyer, or the lawyer is unwilling to sign the affidavit. The latter case normally comes up when a debtor wants to reaffirm a debt that calls for payments he cannot afford to make. The lawyer, therefore, cannot affirm that the agreement does not impose undue hardship on the debtor. In these cases, if the reaffirmation agreement is signed, the court will have a hearing and a judge will decide if the reaffirmation imposes undue hardship and is in the best interests of the debtor. This best interest standard can give the court a little more wiggle room and may cause it to approve a reaffirmation agreement that the lawyer did not feel he or she could sign off on.

The issue of reaffirmations only comes up in Chapter 7 bankruptcies. Within Chapter 7, vehicle loans tend to cause problems. In a Chapter 13 bankruptcy, all unsecured loans are treated the same and vehicles that the debtor retains are normally paid for through the Chapter 13 plan.

In a Chapter 7 filing, the election between reaffirming or not is often harder. In order to qualify for Chapter 7 in the first place, a debtor cannot have meaningful funds left over after covering IRS expenses and secured debt payments. Very often the debtor does not have the income to make secured debt payments such as vehicle payments. On the other hand, a vehicle is needed to get to work, so the debtor wants badly to make an arrangement to keep his or her mode of transportation.

In a perfect world, the debtor would downsize to a less expensive vehicle with lower payments, but because of bad credit many do not have that option. This is why debtors resort to signing reaffirmation agreements their lawyers cannot support.

What happens if I move to another state before I file bankruptcy?

The normal rules of bankruptcy are superseded in two cases when a debtor moves. The first case is rather limited and applies only in those cases that have home exemptions that are in effect unlimited. A debtor may not exempt a residence or homestead that has a value greater than $136,875 (this amount will be adjusted every three years to reflect inflation; hereinafter, *522 limitation*), if that property was acquired by the debtor during the 1,215 days (a little over 3.3 years) prior to filing the bankruptcy.

This rule does not apply to:

1. transfers of interests from the debtor's previous principal residence (which was acquired prior to the beginning of the 1,215 day period) to a new residency, if both residences are located in the same state; or,
2. a family farm which is the principal residence of such farmer.

Even if the above tests are met, the debtor cannot exempt an amount over the 522 limitation if the debtor has been convicted of certain Title 18 felonies or the debtor owes a debt arising from a violation of federal securities laws, or criminal acts, intentional torts, or willful reckless misconducts that caused serious physical injury or death to an individual in the preceding five years.

The second case is by far the more common. It involves debtors who have moved between states in the last 730 days (two years). If a debtor has lived in one state for at least 730 days, you use that state's exemptions. If the debtor has not lived in one state for 730 days, then you use the exemptions of the state where you were domiciled for the longer portion of the 180-day period immediately preceding the 730-day period. For example, Sue lived in Texas and Ohio during the 730-day period prior to filing bankruptcy in Texas. She lived in Ohio for two months of the 180-day period prior to the 730-day period and in New York for one year prior to that. Sue would use New York exemptions in her bankruptcy.

THE DOS AND DON'TS OF FILING FOR BANKRUPTCY

- If I'm considering filing for bankruptcy, what are some things I should avoid doing?
- Why is it a bad idea to pay off loans to family members right before I declare bankruptcy?
- Why is it a bad idea to transfer or sell property to family or friends at a sweetheart price before I declare bankruptcy?
- Why is it a bad idea to pay off car loans just before filing bankruptcy?
- What about buying a new car or a reliable car right before I declare bankruptcy?
- Why is hiding assets a bad idea?

If I'm considering filing for bankruptcy, what are some things I should avoid doing?

Eventually, even the most optimistic person starts to realize that bankruptcy is a real possibility. When this happens, people naturally begin to think of steps they can take to protect their hard-earned property for their families. Some of these steps will merely cause problems when and if bankruptcy is filed, while others may consist of fraud and cause the person to end up in jail.

Common steps people consider are:

- paying off loans to family members and close friends;
- transferring or selling property to family or friends at a low price;
- paying off their car loans;
- buying a new car or reliable car; and,
- hiding assets.

Why is it a bad idea to pay off loans to family members right before I declare bankruptcy?

Payments to family members are specifically forbidden by the bankruptcy code. In fact, any payment to insiders, such as family, within a two-year period can be recaptured by the trustee.

But this can trap you when you have a practice of making monthly payments to your family members for a loan they made to you. Let's say you borrowed $10,000 from your parents a year ago. Since then, you have paid $500 back to them each month as a loan repayment, which means you have paid a total of $6,000 back to them. The trustee can go to your parents and make them give the $6,000 back to the trustee to be paid out to other creditors. The terrible part of this trap is that often parents have borrowed against their homes or their retirement accounts to make the loan. They do not have the $6,000 to pay back, and if the child can't pay them back, they risk losing their home or a large part of their retirement.

Because repayments to parents have such negative consequences, you should never borrow money from family members when it is money they cannot afford to simply write off. Borrowing from your family when you face hard times seems like a good idea. They will lend to you when often no one else will. But it is a terrible trap if they can't afford to write off any money they lent you. Note that you get the same result if you are giving money to your family.

Why is it a bad idea to transfer or sell property to family or friends at a sweetheart price before I declare bankruptcy?

A closely allied temptation when considering bankruptcy is to sell or transfer goods to family members. When people begin to realize the limited scope of property that can be protected, their first thought is to simply get it out of their name. This is often done with noble interest. For example, a child's car may have been put in his or her parent's name for insurance purposes, or because the child could not qualify for the loan when it was purchased. Everyone knows it was the child's car, because he or she paid for it, but for whatever reason it was never legally put in his or her name. When the parents file bankruptcy and the car title is in the parents' name, it is considered their property and subject to being taken by the bankruptcy court. Often debtors feel it is unfair that the child will lose his or her car because of a legal technicality. Thus people want to transfer the car title to the child where it really should be. Unfortunately, doing this is forbidden by the bankruptcy code.

Bankruptcy is a maze of technicalities and taking steps to fix the facts are a bad idea. The facts as you and your family understand them can rapidly cause large problems in bankruptcy. The sale of property for too low a price to a family member or friend or simply giving it to them can lead both you and the other party into real trouble. The bankruptcy forms ask about such transactions, and you will be faced with the decision to reveal them or to lie.

To tell the truth will cause the transaction to be undone and likely cause heightened review of your whole case by the trustee. If you lie, it is bankruptcy fraud and exposes you to a criminal conviction for a federal crime. It is far better to work your way through the bankruptcy with the facts as you have them when you started having money problems.

Why is it a bad idea to pay off car loans just before filing bankruptcy?

Cars and what to do about them are a fruitful source of missteps for people who are having money problems. Many people, after a little research or asking around, come to the understanding that the bankruptcy laws allow them to keep a car. So they pay off their car shortly before seeing a lawyer, or they continue to make regular car payments, as they always have, and now own their car free and clear.

This is as bad as having too much equity in a house. Take a look at your state's exemption for a motor vehicle. You will be shocked. Most exemptions are in the $2,000–$4,000 range. If the car has a value above your state exemption, then you must either give the car up—and receive back the money equal to the state exemption where it is sold—or pay the difference—assuming you can raise the money to pay the difference from family or friends. You are in effect paying for the vehicle twice. Once, when you paid for it originally, and a second time to the trustee in order to be allowed to keep it.

It is far better to owe money on your car as this will reduce its value. Say you have a vehicle worth $10,000. If you own it free and clear, you would have to pay an amount equal to $10,000 less your state exemption in order to keep it. However, if you owed $9,000 on the car, you would only have a value of $1,000. That is probably within your state's protected zone for vehicles, and you would need to pay nothing to the trustee. (Of course, you would still need to pay the vehicle's lien holder, or they could take the vehicle.)

What about buying a new car or a reliable car right before I declare bankruptcy?

The mirror image of having a car that is paid for can also present a trap in bankruptcy. When people have an old, unreliable car and start to have money problems and consider bankruptcy, they may realize that the car is not likely to last the several years that a Chapter 13 will take. They will have a hard time finding someone to sell them a more reliable vehicle once they have filed bankruptcy. They may even have a little money on hand that they want to transform into something that can be protected in bankruptcy. So they buy a replacement car, the last major purchase they'll make for years.

There are several potential traps in bankruptcy for this type of action. If the money is used to pay for all or most of the vehicle, you have created too much equity in the vehicle, and you may lose it. If you file bankruptcy too soon after you purchase the vehicle, the exemption will not be available. Always check with a lawyer before you take this step. And if you are in the process of filling out the paper work for a bankruptcy, be doubly sure to talk to your bankruptcy lawyer about this. It is amazing how many people will buy cars while in the process of having the bankruptcy papers drawn up and never think to talk to the lawyer about it.

Why is hiding assets a bad idea?

The most dangerous course of action when bankruptcy is near or is being filed is to hide assets. This can range from giving gold rings to a family member to hold, to not listing land owned in another state or country. As with taxes, this type of fraud is hard to spot, so the government has made punishment very severe: perpetrators are often sent to jail.

How does the government find out about it? Ex-spouses, ex-friends, and coworkers. It is amazing how much secretaries know. Creditors have lists of all the things you said you owned when you were trying to get your loan and do not look kindly on you trying to stiff them by hiding these assets while in bankruptcy.

Part II:
Types of Bankruptcy

Section 13

CHAPTER 7 BANKRUPTCY

- What has changed about Chapter 7 bankruptcy?
- What is an automatic stay?
- What is a trustee, and what does he or she do?
- What is a Section 341 meeting?
- What problems can come up when the trustee reviews a bankruptcy petition?
- Will creditors come to the 341 meeting?
- Who else might come to the 341 meeting?
- What happens after the 341 meeting?
- What types of problems arise at the 341 meeting?
- How does the bankruptcy system treat tax refunds received after filing bankruptcy?
- How does the bankruptcy system treat inheritances received after filing?
- What happens if I forget to list something in my bankruptcy petition?
- Are there other problems I should be aware of?

What has changed about Chapter 7 bankruptcy?

Under the old law, there were few restraints to filing a Chapter 7 bankruptcy. Now, in effect, to file a Chapter 7, a person or couple must prove that meaningful repayment of debts is not possible. This is done by passing a means test. The test looks at the average income from all sources over the last six months. Of course, both spouses' incomes are counted if both spouses file for bankruptcy. If only one files, the other spouse's income must still be counted, subject to some setoffs.

What counts as income and what is a setoff is subject to complex, changing rules that can vary from one part of the country to another. These new rules are so complex that they have caused many lawyers to stop doing bankruptcy work.

The means test is worked out in the form STATEMENT OF CURRENT MONTHLY INCOME AND MEANS TEST CALCULATION, which must be filled out. It will walk a given case's numbers through the incomes and setoffs to come up with what can be paid to creditors. The mindset of Congress is that people can pay creditors in a Chapter 13; thus, this is the form's presumption.

Several other steps are now required. A CERTIFICATE OF CREDIT COUNSELING must be filed. The credit counseling must be done before you file. After you file, you must take another financial counseling class and file a CERTIFICATE OF FINANCIAL MANAGEMENT COURSE.

The car industry successfully lobbied to put into the new law that almost everyone who owes money on a vehicle must sign and file with the court a REAFFIRMATION AGREEMENT for each vehicle debt or risk having their vehicle taken by the vehicle creditor. In most cases, these must be reviewed and approved by the court. This creates something of a problem. To file a Chapter 7, one must show via the means test he or she has very little money left over. But to keep one's car, one must show he or she has enough money to pay for the car. Often, a person has a very narrow door he or she is trying to pass through.

What is an automatic stay?

For many people, one of the main reasons they file bankruptcy is to stop phone calls from creditors. The automatic stay is what accomplishes this.

An *automatic stay* is a court order forbidding contact with the debtor by the creditor. The creditors are ordered to stop collection phone calls, letters, and lawsuits. Because of the dangers of legal action against them, most creditors stop all contacts with the debtor. This can be a problem for people who plan to keep on paying off a given debt and depend on the creditor sending them a coupon or reminder each month. The monthly statements stop coming and often people get into trouble with the creditor for not making timely payments on items they wish to keep.

If a creditor wants to continue to try and foreclose on your home, he or she must go to court and ask the judge to lift the stay. This is often granted in a Chapter 7 case. In a Chapter 13 case, though, it is much harder for the creditor to have an automatic stay lifted.

What is a trustee, and what does he or she do?

Once your petition is filed, it is given to a trustee for your case. The *trustee's* job is to represent the creditors in general and obtain as much money as he or she can from you to be paid to your creditors. Your lawyer will use the exemptions your state provides to protect as much of your property and assets as possible.

Most of the trustee's review of your case is done in the trustee's office. In the typical case, your only contact with the trustee will be at the Section 341 meeting, which takes places about a month after you file. There, the trustee will ask you a short series of questions with two purposes in mind. They're seeking your affirmation, under oath, that you put a proper value on all listed property, that you listed all your property, and that you have not improperly transferred money or property to a third person. They will also ask questions about how you came up with the listed value for your home, car, and other property.

What is a Section 341 meeting?

The *Section 341 meeting* is often called a *meeting of creditors* or *first meeting of creditors* as this is the creditors' chance to ask questions. The ringmaster of the meeting of creditors is the bankruptcy trustee. He or she is picked, normally on a rotating basis, from a panel of trustees for the court district. The panel trustees are experienced bankruptcy lawyers. They are not paid much for handling the case, and normally they are undertaking to handle a great many routine, low-paying cases for the opportunity to work on a case that has enough assets to generate a larger fee for the trustee. The trustee is liable for oversight to be sure he or she does a complete and timely job.

What problems can come up when the trustee reviews a bankruptcy petition?

Before you are questioned at the meeting of creditors, the trustee's office will have reviewed your petition to be sure that a fair value has been placed on listed assets, for assets that have a value in excess of the protected zone provided in your state, and for recent financial dealing. The latter includes payments to creditors—especially family members—just before the Chapter 7 petition was filed and the giving or selling of property close to the filing. If a trustee finds you have improperly transferred property to a creditor or family member, he or she can force the recipient to return the property.

Two situations often develop. A parent has title, often for insurance purposes, for a car that is really the child's. The parent transfers the title to the child just before filing bankruptcy to get the legal car title in alignment with the true facts. Another common situation is that a young adult has borrowed money from his or her parents and each month makes a payment toward repaying the loan. In both of these cases, the trustee can force the recipient of the property or the money to *disgorge* (give up) what they have received from the debtor. The value received is used to pay a fee to the trustee and is divided among other creditors.

The trustee does not normally get involved with property you choose to surrender to a creditor. He or she will merely tell you or your lawyer to make arrangements with the creditor to deliver the property or make it available for pickup, if you have not already done so.

Will creditors come to the 341 meeting?

Most creditors will not bother to come and ask questions. However, there is no rule forbidding them from doing so. A creditor may ask about statements concerning assets and income you made on loan applications. This can be very embarrassing and troublesome if the statements on the loan application are different from what is listed on your bankruptcy petition.

The questions asked by the trustee and creditors are normally low-key. People's fears of being cross-examined the way they see in trials on TV do not come to pass. To start with, the format of conducting many cases in a short period of time does not allow lengthy questions. Second, there is normally not much need for extended questioning, as the information on the petition is accurate and complete, and the careful loan applicant will have put a fair value on all property in the loan application.

The atmosphere is much more casual than a trial. There is no judge present. Normally the trustee, the petitioner, and his or her lawyer sit fairly close to each other. There are not all the many extra court officials one sees in a typical trial.

Who else might come to the 341 meeting?

People always ask if there will be other people at the meeting, as they fear having their personal affairs put on public display. There will be other people at the meeting, but almost all of them will be other people who have filed bankruptcy, lawyers, and a few representatives of creditors. We have never seen members of the general public at a meeting of creditors, the way you sometimes see at a state court trial. The meetings of creditors are too boring and out of the way to attract bystanders.

What happens after the 341 meeting?

In the vast majority of Chapter 7 cases, the hearing marks the last step in the process that involves the petitioner. The petitioner then waits about three months to receive his or her discharge letter.

There may be some ministerial steps. The filer may elect to reaffirm some debts. The normal reason to do this is to keep property, such as cars, on which the creditor has a lien and which a creditor could take. You should get the advice of your lawyer before signing such documents.

Following the meeting of creditors there is a short period of suspense, while you wait to see if any of your creditors will challenge you or otherwise cause problems. They have sixty days from the date of the first scheduled meeting of creditors in which to challenge the discharge of their debt. The sixty-day date is called the *bar date*, as it bars creditors from raising objections after that date.

If nothing untoward happens, you should receive your discharge papers about three to five months after you file your petition. (The difference in time will depend on how fast the court system can do its paperwork.) This letter normally states that you have received a bankruptcy discharge. It does not state which debts are discharged. For this reason, it is important to hold on to both your copy of the bankruptcy petition (which lists your creditors) and the discharge letter. They are two halves of the whole. One shows what debts were listed, and the other says that the listed debts are discharged. If your lawyer did not give you a copy of your bankruptcy petition, be sure to ask for one.

What types of problems arise at the 341 meeting?

In the great majority of cases, the meeting of creditors goes smoothly, and all the petitioner needs do is wait for his or her discharge papers. But sometimes problems do come up. One has already been mentioned—transfers to family members within two years prior to the petition being filed. Another is large payments to one creditor within a short time of filing the petition. The system does not want one creditor favored over another. Thus if you made, say, a $1,000 payment to credit card X for one reason or another and paid nothing to the others, the trustee may force credit card X to disgorge the money.

How does the bankruptcy system treat tax refunds received after filing bankruptcy?

Depending on when the petition is filed, the petitioner may be entitled to or receive a tax refund within six months of filing the petition. The trustee and creditors are entitled to this money if it cannot be protected using the exemptions available in the applicable state, a rather unpleasant surprise for many petitioners.

How does the bankruptcy system treat inheritances received after filing?

Inheritances are another possible problem. If people are surprised to learn that the trustee has a potential claim on tax refunds, they are shocked and dismayed to learn that the trustee can take inheritances that accrue within six months of filing. In addition to the loss of a loved one, the person is faced with the loss of property the family member spent a lifetime acquiring. This is a disaster, as the protecting exemptions allowed by state and federal law typically do not come close to protecting what has been inherited. If an inheritance occurs, the trustee will take enough of the petitioner's share of the estate to pay all filed claims and pay for his or her time. Occasionally, the inherited money is sufficiently large to allow for a return of some of the money to the filer after all claims and administrative expenses have been paid, but this does not happen often.

Logically, the petitioner is not much worse off than he or she would have been if he or she had inherited the money the week before filing the bankruptcy petition. In such case, he or she would have paid off the debts and have kept what was left. And he or she may be better off, for often his or her share of the inheritance is not large enough to pay off the debts. But people often do not see it that way. They tend to mentally divide the money into different pots. This pot is the debts, and it has to get along on its own. The other pot is the family inheritance, and it is viewed as a one-time thing, and is his or hers only. They think about the improvements they could make to their homes, education payments for children, or dream vacations. Thus, it is very painful to lose the money that would have paid for these things.

What happens if I forget to list something in my bankruptcy petition?

Sometimes in the stress and rush of preparing the bankruptcy petition, a person will find that he or she forgot to list a debt or an asset. This can be easily overcome, if it is discovered shortly after filing the petition, by adding an amendment to the petition. If it is found later, it can be a larger problem. The trustee or a creditor may conclude you were trying to hide the asset. And if the case has been closed without a creditor being listed, you might not have that debt discharged. Normally, only creditors listed in the bankruptcy have their debts done away with. Even in such a case, there may be ways around this, but it is far better and safer to be very thorough when you supply information for the court in the original filing.

Are there other problems I should be aware of?

Depending on the policies of your creditors, there may be a few unpleasant surprises in store for you. Sometimes hospitals will refuse to release medical information because their debt was discharged in a bankruptcy. Other times creditors, or someone who purchased the debt, will try to collect on a debt that was listed and discharged in a bankruptcy. Lenders may refuse to grant a loan until you prove that a given debt was discharged in your bankruptcy. (This often occurs because the credit report is not complete or correct.) Most of these problems can be overcome if you are careful to hold on to your discharge letter and petition.

For more post-filing problems in Chapter 7 bankruptcy, see Section 17.

Section 14

CHAPTER 11 BANKRUPTCY

- What is a Chapter 11 bankruptcy?
- What legal steps are involved in a Chapter 11?
- What is the committee of creditors?
- What are independent reports?
- What is a disclosure statement?
- What is a plan of reorganization?

What is a Chapter 11 bankruptcy?

When people start to think about bankruptcy, often the first type of bankruptcy that comes to mind is a Chapter 11 bankruptcy. This is likely because they have seen it talked about on TV.

Chapter 11 bankruptcies are newsworthy because they are used by airlines, steel companies, and other large companies when they have financial problems. A Chapter 11 has many legal steps, complex requirements, and is a very expensive undertaking. As such, it is too expensive for almost all private people, or even small business owners.

The goal of a Chapter 11 bankruptcy filing is to stop the business's destructive spiral. It gives everyone time to collect facts to see if the company, perhaps on a greatly stripped-down level, can continue to operate, or whether it should be *liquidated* (all assets sold) in an orderly manner.

In a business, the firm often has a great deal more value than the sum of its assets. Often business equipment brings very little when sold. This is because the assets of most businesses are so specialized that they cannot be used for other purposes by other businesses. In addition, of course, the *goodwill* and *trade name* are lost if the business is shut down. Society and the stakeholders in the business—employees, customers, creditors, and even owners—will achieve the best value if the business can be kept alive.

Sometimes a Chapter 11 is used to avoid unwise contracts that have become an unbearable drag on the company's chance for profitability. This may be a vendor contract or leases. In other cases, there is a desire to sell the business assets or operation as an ongoing business. The Chapter 11 can give you time to dispose of the business in an orderly way. The filing prevents one or two creditors from destroying the business by seizing key property or assets.

What legal steps are involved in a Chapter 11?

There are several distinct legal steps in a Chapter 11 proceeding. First, just like any other bankruptcy, a petition must be filed. This brings the individual or corporation under the protection of the bankruptcy system. Normally the owners or management will want to continue to run the business as *debtor in possession*. The court has the final say over whether or not this will be allowed, but normally the interests of everyone are served by having the people who best know the business continue to operate it.

However, because the business and its property have come under the jurisdiction of the court, reports are typically required to give a running account of what is being done by the debtor in possession and in particular how assets are being disposed of. This often means filing a monthly report with the court, and this can be a hard burden on anyone but a large business.

What is the committee of creditors?

The creditors cannot be disregarded after the filing. The system provides for the creation of one or more *committees of creditors*. These are small groups that represent the creditors in general. This small group is often a big help to businesses who have thousands of creditors to deal with but may not be very helpful to an individual or a small business that has only a few creditors to begin with.

There is a meeting of creditors where the debtor has the opportunity to explain his or her situation—what went wrong and how the future of the business can be protected.

What are independent reports?

Often an independent party is appointed to study the business and give an independent report on its problems and prospects. The petitioner is typically expected to pay the fees of this independent party.

What is a disclosure statement?

A *disclosure statement* must be prepared, which, after approval by the court, will be sent to creditors as a part of the next legal step—solicitations for acceptance of the plan of reorganization. The disclosure statement gives a summary of the plan of reorganization and how the different types of creditors will be treated. A general overview of the finances of the filing entity are given in the disclosure statement, as well as an assessment of what would happen if other alternatives, such as complete liquidation, were followed.

The statement also alerts the reader to risk factors involved in the different alternatives facing the business or person. A hearing on the disclosure statement is held before it and the plan of reorganization can be sent to interested parties. Because the disclosure statement summarizes the plan of reorganization, the plan of reorganization must be thought out early in the process.

What is a plan of reorganization?

The heart of a Chapter 11 is the plan of reorganization. It spells out how each different class of creditor is to be treated. A class is one or more creditors who share similar situations. Part of the art of doing a Chapter 11 is knowing how the different creditors can be put in one or more classes as the needs of the situation require. How creditors are classed is very important as a vote of creditors on the plan will be taken and approval of different classes must be obtained.

The ideal is the approval of every class that is *impaired*, or is receiving less than what is owed them. This of course may not happen, and in that case the court can *cram down* their interest—make them take less if some technical rules are followed. Because a vote of a majority of the members of a given class is required for approval by that class, the makeup of the different classes is very important.

It is a mistake to blindly put together a plan for reorganization and put it to a vote without having a pretty good idea of how key classes will vote. In this way, if you see a group of creditors that does not like a provision, you have the chance to change your proposal before it is written up and mailed out.

Normally, in addition to asking what the creditors think, the debtor and his or her lawyer will negotiate with the creditors about the treatment of their class. Often the creditor must be educated as to what the alternatives are. No creditor likes receiving less than what was contracted for, so the creditor must be made to see that accepting the proposal with its economic loss is better than any of the alternatives.

Often this disintegrates into a game where the creditor has the option to try to kill the reorganization by voting against the plan. They use this power to try to force better terms. The debtor wants the business to keep on operating; that is why he or she filed a Chapter 11. But the plan must leave the debtor a reasonable chance to succeed. Agreeing to an unrealistic plan provision that will surely kill the plan does not help anyone at all.

CHAPTER 13 BANKRUPTCY

- What is a Chapter 13 bankruptcy?
- How does a Chapter 13 operate?
- What are the parts of a Chapter 13 petition?
- What is the proposed plan?
- What happens after the plan is filed?
- Do I still own my property after I file a Chapter 13?
- What happens if I want to sell property after I file a Chapter 13?
- Are people in a Chapter 13 allowed to obtain additional debt?
- What happens if my car is totaled while I am in Chapter 13?
- What happens if my insurance lapses?
- What happens if I have a drop in income?

What is a Chapter 13 bankruptcy?

A Chapter 13 bankruptcy as filed is a hybrid between a Chapter 7 and a Chapter 11. The typical Chapter 13 filer has one or more of three motivations. An important reason for many people is that the creditors may receive back some of the money they loaned you. "I made these debts, and I have always paid my debts," is a common statement from people who file for Chapter 13 bankruptcy. People are willing to put up with the problems inherent in the Chapter 13 process out of the moral or psychological wish to pay back at least some of their debts.

Another reason people file Chapter 13 is to save their homes or cars. Unlike a Chapter 7, a Chapter 13 is designed to stop foreclosures and repossessions. The creditor can object if the proposed Chapter 13 repayment plan is unrealistic or if the property will depreciate faster than the creditor is paid under the plan. However, given a reasonable plan, a Chapter 13 program will allow a debtor a chance to save his or her home and car and make up missed payments a little each month.

This latter factor is very important in dealing with homes. Many Chapter 13 filers are people who, for one reason or another, missed monthly house payments. Often the creditor's response is to demand that all back payments be made as a lump sum, and they refuse to take offered monthly payments. If a person can't pay all back payments at once, his or her only option may be to file a Chapter 13. The other options, refinancing the home or debt consolidation loans, typically are not available because of the black mark on the debtor's credit caused by the missed house payments.

A third reason people file Chapter 13 is that it affords them the chance to retain property they would lose in a Chapter 7. Chapter 7 filers have the possibility of losing property, if their property is worth more than the value allowed as an exemption. This is a common occurrence in every state. Much of this property can be protected in a Chapter 13. As long as creditors receive at least as much as they would have received in a Chapter 7, the Chapter 13 will work. The amount the creditors receive does not need to be paid all at once as would be the case in a Chapter 7. The payment can be stretched out over the three- to five-year life of the Chapter 13.

How does a Chapter 13 operate?

A form very much like the means test must be filled out as part of filing the Chapter 13. It is used to work out the size and term (three to five years) of the plan. Its long name is STATEMENT OF CURRENT MONTHLY INCOME AND CALCULATION OF COMMITMENT PERIOD AND DISPOSABLE INCOME. It looks at average income from all sources for the last six months. Both spouses' incomes are counted, subject to some setoffs for the nonfiling spouse.

What is income and what is setoff is subject to complex, changing rules that can vary from one part of the country to another. The debtor(s) must also receive credit counseling before they file, as a CERTIFICATE OF CREDIT COUNSELING must be filed with the petition.

What are the parts of a Chapter 13 petition?

The structure of a Chapter 13 petition is similar to a Chapter 7 petition. It has ten schedules, comprehensive catalogs of your income, assets, and debts. Additionally, it has a proposed plan, which sets out how debts are to be paid. The petition also includes a statement of financial affairs. The schedules are organized as follows.

Schedule A	Real Property
Schedule B	Personal Property
Schedule C	Property claimed as exempt
Schedule D	Secured creditors
Schedule E	Priority creditors
Schedule F	Unsecured creditors
Schedule G	Executory contracts and unexpired leases
Schedule H	Codebtors
Schedule I	Current income
Schedule J	Current expenses

What is the proposed plan?

The heart of the Chapter 13 is the *proposed plan*, which sets out how each class of creditors will be paid. It is similar to a Chapter 11 plan, but less complex, as it is dealing with a wage earning individual or an individual who operates a small business rather than a large, complex business.

It will set out how long the plan will last—three to five years—and what will be paid to the trustee and to the lawyer who represented the debtor. It will then list how the different main classes of creditors will be paid. Secured creditors may either be paid in full or partially paid in full and partially paid as unsecured creditors. Debtors may choose to pay cosigned claims in full to protect the cosigners.

The plan will state how back taxes and student loans will be treated and will set out how fast arrearages (missed payments) will be repaid. The plan will also state in a general way how the unsecured claims—credit cards, personal loans, medical bills, etc.—will be treated. This is the plug number in most plans as there is often a general understanding in a given area about what percentage must be paid to unsecured general creditors. If the proposed plan is too aggressive in limiting what is paid to creditors, they can object and a court hearing will be held.

Two overarching constraints limit the plan. First, the unsecured creditors must receive at least what they would have received in a Chapter 7 bankruptcy. Second, the debtor must devote all or substantially all of his or her disposable income to the repayment plan. Disposable income is money available from income after reasonable living expenses are deducted. This opens another avenue for disputes as a creditor or trustee may have an objection stating that a given debtor's living expenses are not reasonable. It was thought that this area of dispute would be done away with by the IRS living standards budget and the means test, but they still occur.

Areas of dispute in addition to the normal cost of food and entertainment issues are expenses for charitable giving, repayment of loans against retirement plans, and the cost of private schooling for the debtor's children. The plan will also state which creditors are to be paid directly, what property is to be surrendered, and which executory contracts and leases will be kept or given up.

What happens after the plan is filed?

A first meeting of creditors is held where creditors can question the debtor, and then there is time allowed for the creditors to object to the plan. At the time of filing, the creditors are notified to file their claims with the court stating how much they believe they are owed. It is not uncommon for this amount to be different from what the debtor claims he or she owes. The debtor can object to the claim if he or she thinks it is incorrect. A hearing would then be held to see which party is correct.

If there are no objections by any party, the plan goes into effect as written and is binding on all parties.

Do I still own my property after I file a Chapter 13?

A Chapter 13 plan lasts for three to five years, and during that time the debtor has a special relationship with the court. In a Chapter 7 filing, the trustee takes what property he or she can and sells it. In a Chapter 13, the debtor is allowed to keep and use the property but is accountable to the court for its use. He or she is treated as a debtor in possession of bankruptcy property, or debtor in possession. Because the court could have taken the property to settle debts but did not, the debtor must stand ready to account for this property.

What happens if I want to sell property after I file a Chapter 13?

The main time this debtor-in-possession theory causes a problem is when people want to sell their home or their vehicles. Because it is the property of the bankruptcy estate, you are not free to just sell the property and pocket the money. You must first obtain permission of the court for the sale and account for the money received. By the same token, you cannot, for example, just give a vehicle to your child because everyone in the family knows it is really the child's car.

Are people in a Chapter 13 allowed to obtain additional debt?

While you are under Chapter 13, you are not allowed to incur more debt. This means you must stop charging on credit cards and cannot borrow money during the life of the plan without the court's or trustee's specific permission. This often causes problems when cars wear out or when the debtor must move.

Before the court will allow new or additional debt, it will want to know the terms of the new debt, what is being bought, and why. The court wants to be sure the additional debt can be repaid without hurting the old creditors.

What happens if my car is totaled while I am in Chapter 13?

A problem that is fairly common during the life of the Chapter 13 plan is a car wreck. Sometimes it seems that car wrecks seek out people in Chapter 13. In a certain number of these wrecks the debtor's car will be totaled. This means the debtor must replace the car and will need new financing. The system allows for this financing to be done by the old lien holder, if there is one, with the old lien holder obtaining a lien on the new car.

In practice this can be a problem. If your car is totaled, the insurance company often does not pay enough to replace the car. The creditor, if it is to substitute collateral, will want a car at least as valuable as the one that was wrecked and does not care that the insurance payoff was not enough to purchase such a car. Often the creditor will refuse to allow any substitution on collateral, and the debtor must ask for help from the court. All of this takes time, and you may very well have to pay extra to obtain the replacement car. This is very hard on debtors who are without a car to drive to work and already short of ready cash.

What happens if my insurance lapses?

When a person takes out a loan on a car, a standard clause in his or her loan agreement requires him or her to keep *collision insurance*. This will allow the lender to recover some of the loaned money if something happens to the car.

Once in Chapter 13, people often have a hard time making ends meet. They may have suffered a drop in income or have agreed to a repayment plan they really could not quite afford in an effort to save a home or car. To make ends meet there is a temptation to let insurance premiums slide.

This is a mistake. The creditor has the ability to repossess cars if you fail to keep insurance on them, as required by the security agreement. The idea behind this is that the creditor is being kept by the bankruptcy filing from taking the car, and in exchange you have a duty to give the creditor the protection offered by the collision insurance policy.

What happens if I have a drop in income?

The short answer is that you are expected to make the Chapter 13 monthly payment whether or not you have a shortfall in a given month because of decreased income or higher expenses. Sometimes the trustee will give you a chance to make up a short payment. However, this is often not much help. You will be expected to make increased payments until the shortfall is made up in a short period of time. Often people find themselves in a sort of downward spiral. They could not pay their payment of X and now they must pay X plus an amount to make up the missed payment. Unless the shortfall was a one-time blip this may be impossible and the debtor will be dropped from the Chapter 13 program.

Section 16

POST-FILING ISSUES

- How are inheritances treated?
- How are tax refunds treated?
- How is money from divorce or separation decrees, property settlements, or property earnings treated?
- How are gifts from friends and family treated?
- Why is it a bad idea not to report tax refunds or inheritances to the trustee?
- How are income increases treated?
- How can increases in income come to the attention of the Chapter 13 trustee?

How are inheritances treated?

As previously stated, in a Chapter 7 proceeding, money you inherit within six months after you file your petition is subject to being taken by the trustee for benefit of creditors. This is always a terrible shock to people in addition to the sadness of the loss of a loved one—normally a parent. The filer stands to lose much of what his or her family member worked so hard to build up. The general rules of exemptions apply to inheritances, but usually inheritances are so large that the exemption protection does not help much.

In a Chapter 13, receiving an inheritance runs into two problems. The first is the general rule that creditors in a Chapter 13 should receive at least what creditors in a Chapter 7 would have received. The second is the *disposable income test*. People in a Chapter 13 are supposed to devote all of their disposable income to the Chapter 13 plan. If you inherit money, this means you have more to pay your creditors with.

How are tax refunds treated?

The same general rules apply to tax refunds above your protected limit. Here the wild card, exemptions in any asset allowed if you did not use your homestead exemption, may be useful. A $2,000 protection zone may not be very helpful in the case of an inheritance, but could be enough to protect a major portion of a tax refund. In a multiyear Chapter 13 plan, tax refunds do not normally come into consideration.

How is money from divorce or separation decrees, property settlements, or property earnings treated?

In Chapter 7 proceedings, money you gain within six months of filing your petition is subject to being taken by the trustee. In many states, property held by a couple is protected. But it loses this protection when the couple divorces or goes through legal separation. If a state allows wild card exemptions, these can be used to protect part of the assets.

In a Chapter 13, how these funds are treated if you obtain a right to them during the life of your plan will depend on the trustee. Normally, the trustee will be interested in collecting these funds for the benefit of your creditors.

How are gifts from friends and family treated?

Money you receive as a gift from your family after filing a bankruptcy is normally protected. This means that a family member or friend could purchase a car or other items for you. In many cases, such people buy items and property from the trustee as part of the sale of assets procedure.

Why is it a bad idea not to report tax refunds or inheritances to the trustee?

The trustee learning about your inheritance or tax refund depends to a great extent on the honor system. There is not a central repository that lists inheritances or tax refunds. The trustee may never know about the inheritance or tax refund if you do not tell him or her. This creates a strong incentive to cheat the system by never telling anyone about it.

Not revealing assets such as inheritances and tax refunds is a bankruptcy crime, and people who hide assets are subject to federal criminal prosecution. You could go to jail. Do not expect your lawyer to help you hide these assets. Lawyers are forbidden to help people commit a crime.

How are income increases treated?

In a Chapter 7 bankruptcy filing, most of the time good fortune that befalls you after you file bankruptcy is good fortune that does not need to be shared. If you land a new, higher-paying job or get a raise in your present job, the increase is yours. The idea of the Chapter 7 bankruptcy is to give you a fresh start in life. If the creditors or the bankruptcy system could reach out and seize property as you are trying to rebuild your life, this purpose would be defeated.

A Chapter 13 proceeding can be different. In a Chapter 7 filing, a snapshot of one's financial affairs is taken the day you file, and that is basically all there is to it. But, in a Chapter 13, you subject yourself and your property to the review of the court for several years. This gives time for the disposable income test to bite you. Some Chapter 13 courts, trustees, and creditors will take the position that if you are earning more money, then you have more disposable income to pay to your creditors and may push for a larger payment. Normally, this is not a problem. As your income rises your reasonable living expenses will also increase. The net result is that no more disposable income is available for creditors.

How can increases in income come to the attention of the Chapter 13 trustee?

It is not uncommon for a person in Chapter 13 to need to buy another car or a new house during the three to five years the Chapter 13 plan lasts. To undertake new indebtedness to purchase a car or house requires the permission of the court or trustee. This permission will not be forthcoming unless the person can afford it.

People will then reveal their higher income in an effort to show they can afford the requested purchase. With this information in front of them, the court, trustee, or creditor then invokes the disposable income rule. In a few cases, the people end up being turned down for the house or car and are required to pay more into the plan because of higher disposable income.

POST-FILING STEPS AND PROBLEMS IN CHAPTER 7

- If I file bankruptcy, will there be an audit of my possessions?
- Can creditors challenge my bankruptcy petition?
- Can my bankruptcy petition be challenged by third parties?
- Can I suffer criminal sanctions if I try to hide my assets?

Note: A great deal of trust is placed on the person who fills out the bankruptcy petition, but the system provides for chances to test the truthfulness of the filer. One step is a meeting, called the Section 341 meeting, discussed in Section 13.

If I file bankruptcy, will there be an audit of my possessions?

If there are questions about the filing, the trustee can order an audit. This can take several forms. The trustee may, but normally does not, direct an appraiser to go out to a person's home and value the contents of the home. This is done when the filer has a very expensive home but puts a very low value on the furnishings in that home. Trustees have found through experience that people with very expensive homes tend to buy expensive, high quality furniture for those homes. They may also send an appraiser to value vehicles. Sometimes old cars are not worth much at all, and sometimes they are a valuable collector's item.

Under the new bankruptcy code, cases are also randomly audited. Every two hundred and fiftieth case is picked for review. The auditors, amongst other things, will request bank statements with explanations of large deposits and withdrawals. This was done to try to ensure honesty in the system. The greater likelihood of obtaining money from a sale makes this expense worthwhile for the trustee.

The audits require you to back up your statements in the bankruptcy petition. If you are audited, you will be asked to produce deeds and car titles—to see what type of car you really own and who owns the land and the vehicle—and bank records to see how much money you really have.

Can creditors challenge my bankruptcy petition?

One of the main safeguards in the system is that creditors or government officials overseeing the case can challenge the petition and the propriety of debt discharge. An important source of challenges is changes in the filer's borrowing and spending pattern. Sometimes people go on spending sprees just before filing their bankruptcy. They take a vacation or buy a large number of personal items. Then they try to do away with these debts through bankruptcy. Creditors have the right to challenge discharge of these debts.

In the past, if a creditor gave an individual a line of credit, it was the creditor's problem if the borrower used it. The idea was to be sure who you were lending to and get security for your loans. Today the rules are a bit different. Borrowers on *standing lines of credit*—such as credit cards—are often deemed to be making a representation of their ability and intent to repay each time they draw or charge on their line of credit. If this representation is found to be false, the creditor can move to not allow the debt to be discharged. Some creditors try to abuse this new power by putting a squeeze play on borrowers. They challenge many charges and leave it up to the borrower to demonstrate their motives were pure when they borrowed.

The problem with this is that the final arbitrator of the borrower's intentions is a judge, and it is expensive to have a federal trial before a judge. This involves many filings and appearances before the court and extensive *discovery* (gathering of evidence). The creditor has deep pockets and the bankrupt defendant is, by definition, without money. Some creditors use this situation to go on fishing expeditions. They threaten challenges and then offer to settle for a lesser sum. If they can threaten enough people and induce them to settle, they can collect a tidy sum across the country.

Creditors will also ask why the assets and their values listed on a loan are different from what is shown on the bankruptcy petition. If a great deal of money or assets have disappeared, they will want to know what happened to it.

Can my bankruptcy petition be challenged by third parties?

Another element that makes the system work is that third parties often call the trustee's attention to improper action by the filer. Unhappy business associates or ex-spouses are a fruitful source of negative information. Ex-employees also often know a lot and will call the trustee's attention to improper actions or assets that have not been listed. (There was even a case where a filer tried to hide assets by buying an expensive exempt asset, filing, and then returning the asset for a refund. The merchant, unhappy at losing the big sale, turned the filer in.)

Can I suffer criminal sanctions if I try to hide my assets?

If it comes out that a filer tried to lie to the trustee or to hide assets, the filer is subject to criminal sanctions of fines and time in jail. Every month brings stories of people fined and sent to prison for trying to hide assets or otherwise beat the system. It's not worth attempting to get away with it.

REBUILDING CREDIT

- Why should I have credit?
- Can I get credit after declaring bankruptcy?
- How long will it take to obtain credit on normal terms after bankruptcy?
- Should I reaffirm credit cards?
- How is my credit score determined?
- How do I get a copy of my credit report?
- How can I get the credit reporting agencies to fix errors on my credit report?
- Why should I check court records?
- How do I go about rebuilding my credit?
- Can I buy better credit?
- Does having a landline phone help my credit?
- Will bank accounts help my credit score?
- Will secured bank loans help my credit score?
- Will secured credit cards help my credit score?
- Why should I even want a credit card?
- Will department store credit cards help my credit score?
- Will car loans help my credit score?
- Can I get a mortgage while rebuilding my credit?
- Can I travel without credit?

Why should I have credit?

Some clients say, "I never want to see another credit card or owe anything." While understandable, this may be an overreaction and counterproductive. While you can exist just fine without a credit card, sooner or later you will need to buy a car or will have to move and buy a new home or rent an apartment. To do any of these things will require a reasonable credit rating. If you do nothing about rebuilding your credit standing, you may not be able to qualify for the car, home, or apartment. Credit is much like a muscle—it needs to be used to be available when needed. So go ahead and work on developing your credit standing and use your credit a little bit. In that way you will build a good credit record should you ever need it.

Can I get credit after declaring bankruptcy?

There is a common misconception that people who have filed bankruptcy can never receive credit again. Rest assured, you can have credit again, it will just take some time and effort. There is too much profit for financial institutions to cut you off from credit for very long.

How long will it take to obtain credit on normal terms after bankruptcy?

It is hard to give a firm rule on how long it will take to receive credit again. There is not a law saying when you are again entitled to credit—it is up to the individual bank or business. And there are millions of banks and creditors in the country. Some are liberal in extending credit. Others will pass up a sale or a loan if you ever filed bankruptcy. All that can be done is to describe averages.

Time is one of your great allies. The longer ago your bankruptcy, the less it will affect you. Most of the time, you should be well on your way back to having a normal credit rating within two to five years. It will go a bit faster if you have been working hard on rebuilding credit. The two- to five-year figure is for mainstream credit cards. It may take longer to get back to an A-rating in applying for a home.

Should I reaffirm credit cards?

It is not easy to obtain new credit. If regaining access to credit takes time and is hard, why not reaffirm some of the debts you had prior to bankruptcy? This will let you keep one or more of your relationships with old lenders. All you have to do is pay off the balance you owe on the debt, and you have a credit card you can charge on, or a loan company to go to for future loans.

Let's discuss the reaffirmation process. Say you owe $2,000 on a credit card. You would sign an agreement, or note in your bankruptcy petition, that you promise to pay the debt in spite of having the right to wipe it out as part of the bankruptcy process. The implied trade-off for your doing this is that you will get to keep the card and use it in the future. However, some credit card issuers will revoke the card once a customer files bankruptcy. So reaffirming the card merely means you have taken forward a debt you did not have to pay and will receive no benefit from your act.

The main reason bankruptcy lawyers counsel against this course of action is that you need to get your financial feet under you before you start using credit again. Another reason is that often people want to reaffirm a larger debt than they can afford to pay given their current financial situation. And remember that often the creditor will cut off your access to its credit line after you reaffirm. You end up owing the debt that you already had discharged in bankruptcy, and you do not have use of the card or line of credit, which puts you in a worse position than you were in before you reaffirmed your credit card debt.

If the bank does not revoke your card, it will almost certainly lower your credit limit to the amount you owe on the card. Thus, if you owe $2,000, then your credit limit is lowered to $2,000. In effect, you cannot use the card to charge anything until you pay off part of the $2,000. And remember, making the minimum payments each month will not make the balance go down much at all. You will need to make monthly payments that are a lot larger than the minimum payment to actually obtain use of the card.

Meanwhile, do not forget you are starting out at your maximum credit limit. It is very easy to slip up and have an over-the-limit charge applied against you. These charges are becoming larger and larger as lenders search for more ways to make money. The fact that you are at your limit because you reaffirmed the debt and had your limit lowered will not make one bit of difference to the computer that is doing the over-the-limit calculations.

The most important reason to think long and hard about reaffirming a credit card debt is that you, in all likelihood, will not be able to pay down the debt fast enough to ever actually use your card. Most people who file Chapter 7 do not have any money left over from their paycheck after their living expenses are deducted. In fact, most have living expenses higher than their monthly income. The factor that allows them to survive month to month is that their insurance and tax payments do not have to be paid each month and clothes are only purchased infrequently.

Taking on another bill may be the straw that breaks your back. If you run into repayment problems on the reaffirmed debt, then you are in real trouble. Having a bad payment history after bankruptcy is worse than having a bad payment history prior to bankruptcy. It shows you have not learned your lesson.

If you do have extra funds left over after paying your living expenses, you can actually afford to pay down a credit card, and you have a real need for credit, then think about reaffirming a debt or two. Choose which one to reaffirm carefully. It is far better to reaffirm a credit card with a $500 limit than one with a $2,000 limit. Your goal is to have a credit card or two to use and rebuild your credit, not to be able to brag about how much credit you have available.

Next, be sure the card you keep is one that reports to the credit bureaus. Some department stores do not report to the credit bureaus. Pick a major credit card—Visa or MasterCard. Those will be reported, and having one can help you get the right department store and gas company credit card when the proper time comes.

How is my credit score determined?

If you are serious about rebuilding your credit in the fastest possible time, you need to learn how your credit rating is determined.

Much of the credit rating in the country is done by a California company named Fair, Isaac, and Company. It licenses its program to determine creditworthiness to the big three credit bureaus and other businesses that may want to determine whether or not to make loans. Fair, Isaac was one of the first and best companies to use complex mathematical algorithms, crunched on computers, to predict borrower's future actions. Developing consumer financial profiles produces a large part of the company's revenue. To protect this income stream, it has tried to keep the factors that are considered in its algorithms and how they are multiplied a secret. For this reason, anyone writing on credit rebuilding prior to June 2000 relied purely on intuition, observation, and guesswork.

Fair, Isaac scores are used by about 75% of the country's mortgage lenders and all three major credit bureaus. Each bureau has its own name for the score, but they are all based on the FICO score (short for Fair, Isaac Company Score). These scores have been used for decades in consumer loan and credit card evaluations under a heavy veil of secrecy. But controversy developed as the score method moved into the mortgage industry. All aspects of people's lives were being controlled by a small group in California, without accountability and in total secrecy.

This raw display of power created a disturbance, and at last state governments and the Federal Trade Commission (FTC) began to consider whether to pass a law to make Fair, Isaac reveal all. In July 1999, Fair, Isaac made a presentation of some of the factors used in determining a consumer's credit score. It gave examples of twelve factors and how differences in them would award different points. The higher the score, the more credit-worthy one is.

Own/Rent	Own	Rent	Other	No Info				
	25	15	10	17				
Years at Address	<0.5	0.5–2.49	2.5–6.49	6.5–10.49	>10.49	No Info		
	12	10	15	19	23	13		
Occupation	Pro	Semi-Pro	Manager	Office	Blue Col	Retired	Other	No Info
	50	44	31	28	25	31	22	27
Years on Job	<0.5	0.5–1.49	1.5–2.49	2.5–5.49	5.5–12.49	12.5	Retired	No Info
	2	8	19	25	30	39	43	20
Depart. Store/ Maj. Cred. Card	None	Dept. Store	Major CC	Both	No Answer	No Info		
	0	11	16	27	10	12		
Bank Reference	Checking	Savings	Check. & Sav.	Other	No Info			
	5	10	20	11	9			
Debt Ratios	<15	15–25	26–35	36–49	50+	No Info		
	22	15	12	5	0	13		
Number Inquiries	0	1	2	3	4	5–9	No Rec.	
	3	11	3	-7	-7	-20	0	

Years in File	<0.5	1–2	3–4	5–7	8+			
	0	5	15	30	40			
Number Revolving Trades	0	1–2	3–5	6+				
	5	12	8	4				
% Balances Available	0–15%	16–30%	31–40%	41–50%	>50%			
	15	5	-3	-10	-18			
Worst Credit Derog	No Record	Any Derog	Any Slow	1 Satisf. Line	2 Satisf. Lines	3 Satisf. Lines		
	0	-29	-14	17	24	29		

The first row in each block is the individual's status. The second row is the points allocated for that status.

For more information, see the FTC website at www.FTC.gov. Clearly these are not all the factors. Fair, Isaac once stated that even a simple credit scoring system is likely to have ten thousand or twenty thousand different possible combinations. The total scores range from three hundred to eight hundred points. So the few elements given in the government briefing cover only a part of the possible score range.

As you look at the sample chart, there are many factors you cannot change in your efforts to rebuild your credit standing. But, there are several things you can do.

- Stay at one address and do not move around.
- When you do obtain credit, make sure you make timely payments.
- If you have a job, stay with the same company.
- If you are running your own business, you may wish to consider taking a part-time job so that your report shows employment with steady income.

How do I get a copy of my credit report?

While working on rebuilding your credit, you will need to keep a sharp eye on your credit report. The FICO score uses information from your credit report so you will want to make sure it is up to date and accurate. Be sure to order a credit report from each of the three major credit reporting agencies as information on them can be different and you never know which one a potential credit extender will use. Their phone numbers are:

Equifax: 800–997–2493

Trans Union: 800–888–4213

Experian: 888–397–3742

The cost for each credit report normally runs about $8. However, if you go to the website www.annualcreditreport.com, you can get one free credit report from each of the three major credit reporting agencies every twelve months.

It is important to review your credit reports at least once a year, because there are often errors on them that can affect your ability to get credit. Common errors include having data for other people in your file, and to not show a debt as paid off or discharged in bankruptcy. Order your credit report and go over it with a fine-tooth comb.

How can I get the credit reporting agencies to fix errors on my credit report?

If there is an error, be sure to immediately write to the reporting agency to correct it. If you have already declared bankruptcy, send a copy of your bankruptcy discharge letter and the list of creditors if a debt is not shown as discharged on your report.

Challenge debts that are not yours or that are wrong. To do this, write to the credit bureau and challenge the history and ask that the entry be researched. By law, the bureau must go back to the reporting company and ask for documentation of the entry. Ideally, the company will look at its records and note the entry is wrong and have it corrected. More likely, the company will not bother to respond. If they do not, the entry must be taken off your credit report.

If you have already declared bankruptcy, even though you'll have to pay for it, you should order another copy of your credit report and score every three to six months. This will allow you to track how your credit rebuilding efforts are working.

Why should I check court records?

Often, people who had court judgments against them have long since paid them off, but the court records do not show it. Most people just assume that once they have paid the debt, the judgment will disappear. This is not the case. The court has no way of knowing if you paid off a judgment or not. For a judgment to be marked satisfied, someone—usually the judgment holder—must advise the court system that the judgment has been paid.

Many creditors simply do not bother to do this. They have their money, which is what they are interested in. To get in touch with the court is extra work that does not produce a profit, so why do it?

It is up to you to be sure that paid-off judgments are removed from the court records. First, check the judgment book at the courthouse for the court that entered the judgment. Be sure each judgment is marked *satisfied*. It is very important to have judgments shown as paid, as any unpaid judgments are automatically picked up by the credit agencies and hurt your credit score.

If a judgment has not been marked as paid, you will need to get in touch with the creditor and have it reported to the court that the judgment was satisfied. Often the best you can get from the creditor is a note that says the judgment was paid. You will have to do the leg work of getting this information to the courthouse.

How do I go about rebuilding my credit?

The first step is to realize that your credit rating is not a reflection of your worth as a person. Rather, a credit rating is only a statement of how likely a lender is to make money off of you. To determine this, they look at several factors. First, are other companies making money off of you? That is, do you have other debts and are you paying them regularly and on time? We cannot overemphasize the importance of paying your bills on time. Second, do you have blemishes on your record—have you had foreclosures, repossessions, bankruptcy, or charge-offs? Third, are you stable? Do you have ties to the community and a regular job? Like a bail bondsman, lenders want to know how likely you are to skip town and how easy you will be to find. Fourth, do you have a regular flow of income? A nice job with a regular income is best. Worst is no job. Somewhere in-between is being self-employed. At best, a self-employed person or small business owner has an irregular income, up some months and years and down in others. When the income is down, it will be hard—if not impossible—to make the regular payments that bankers want.

However, be careful who you go to for credit and how you do it. There is a feeling among people who study the art of rebuilding credit that going to high interest credit cards, subprime markets, or even finance companies will not help you much, and may even hurt you. Therefore, be careful of credit card solicitations you receive while you are in bankruptcy or just after you come out of bankruptcy. These are often high interest, high charge cards.

Can I buy better credit?

Be especially careful of letters offering to obtain a credit card for you for a fee. Often the only thing these companies are interested in is obtaining your fee. They will forward your application on to several credit card companies—often high interest ones. You could do the same thing yourself with a little research. The result—you will be out money you did not need to spend. In addition, you will have a large number of credit inquiries on your credit record (a FICO negative) and will probably end up with only offers to extend credit from a high interest card.

As you apply for credit, be careful in dealing with lenders, so as to avoid getting too many inquiries on your record. What many people do when they want to reestablish their credit standing is send out a number of inquiries and hope that one will be accepted. But, unfortunately, the very act of sending out applications to several lenders lessens your chances of being accepted. Look at line eight on the FICO scoring chart. The lowest score you can get is to have more than five inquiries. The chart does not say over what time period, but you can be sure that many inquiries over a month or so will not look good on your permanent record.

Does having a landline phone help my credit?

While much of a FICO score is beyond your control, there are some things you can affect. One of the first things you should do is have a landline phone in your name. It is not unusual for people during their run to bankruptcy to have their phone service cut off because they were not able to pay their phone bill.

A landline phone in most places is considered a public utility and the company will have to provide your phone service and can cover the credit risk by requiring a deposit. The amount of the deposit will vary. In our area, it is two months average usage. Thus, if your habit was to make a lot of long-distance charges, your deposit will be higher than if you made only local calls. View paying the deposit as a cost of being in the game and pay what is required. Whatever they ask, try to get a phone. Lack of a phone shows a lack of stability, and this will hurt you as you try to rebuild your credit.

Be careful of phone services that cater to people who have had their phone service cut off. Using them will place you in a pool of credit risks and just may work against you. Work on obtaining phone service from your mainline phone company.

Will bank accounts help my credit score?

Make sure you open a bank checking and savings account. Be careful in doing this if you do not already have one, or must move. Many banks will not open a new account for people who have bounced checks. Some banks will not open checking accounts for people who have bad credit. This is not a universal practice, but it does happen on occasion. If you are opening a new account, talk to the bank officer and ask what the bank's policy is. A turn down for a checking or savings account probably will not be reported to the credit bureaus and thus would not hurt you—but why take the chance?

Will secured bank loans help my credit score?

Getting a secured bank loan—and paying it off in full and on time—can help your credit score. After you have a savings and checking account at your bank, start thinking about a secured loan from that bank. This is where you have, say, $500 in your savings account, and you obtain a loan of $400 or $500. The bank will put a lock on your money, so if you do not pay, the loan is fully protected. It might at first seem like this type of loan would be easy to obtain because the bank is protected. But you must keep in mind how loan officers are graded. If they make a loan that goes bad it is a black mark on their record and hurts their chances of promotion. So the loan officer is likely to be careful about making a loan to you. This is another case where you should talk to the bank officer to try to find out ahead of time if he or she will make the loan.

Remember, the bank will request data from the credit bureaus in considering the loan and too many inquiries will hurt you. You want each inquiry to result in a loan. It is extra work to take the time to sit down and talk with the loan officer, but you have had a financial mishap and will probably need to do the work if you want to speed up your credit availability.

Once you have the secured loan, make sure you pay it back on time. Your goal is to have a satisfactory line on your credit report for that loan for the FICO scorekeepers to take into account. We suggest that you do not use the loan at all—bank it so that you will be sure to have the money to pay back the loan as it comes due. You may ask yourself, "If I cannot use the loan, what good is it?" Its purpose is to gain you a good post-bankruptcy rating on your credit report. The interest you pay on the loan is the price you pay for the good entry. You are starting to rebuild a record on lenders making money off of you.

You might even be able to talk the bank into loaning you the money it puts a hold on. This is hard to do, as it seems to go against everything bank officers believe in. But, if you are lucky, you will obviously be able to borrow more and have a higher loan repayment on your record.

Will secured credit cards help my credit score?

Another source of secured loans is secured credit cards. These work in much the same way as a secured bank personal loan. You deposit, for instance, $500 in the bank that issues the secured credit card and your credit limit on the card is $500. Secured credit cards used to be hard to find, but if you have access to the Internet, it is now somewhat easier.

Before you settle on one, ask the bank how long it will be until your credit limit is lifted beyond what you have deposited in their bank. This assumes you have a perfect payment history. Some banks, no matter how well you do, will not give you unsecured credit. Your job is to find the ones that will.

You may receive offers in the mail for secured credit cards. Be very careful in accepting these—going with companies that offer these credit cards can work against you. An easy way to find secured credit cards is through the Internet—but this may not be the best way. This is just another way of making a mass offering—similar to mail solicitations. Be careful.

Before you sign up, call and ask some important questions.

- Do they report to the major credit bureaus, and if so, which ones?
- Do they report your card as a secured credit card? If they do, it will probably not help to rebuild your credit. Even if they say they do not, check up on them. This is one of the things you should review when you order follow up credit reports.
- How long is your grace period on monthly payments? Too short a grace period will cause you to pay extra interest. The worst is interest accruing from the date of charge.
- Is there an application fee? The lower the fee, the better.
- What is the minimum and maximum deposit required or allowed in setting up an account? A low balance can create just as successful a payment entry as a high one.
- With a good payment history, how long will it take to be changed into an unsecured credit card? Aim for twelve to eighteen months.
- What is the interest rate on outstanding balances? Some banks will charge a very high interest rate. All other things being equal, lower is better.

- Is there an annual service fee? None or low is better but hard to find.
- Do they pay interest on the security deposit that is made?
- Do they deal with people in your state? Some banks will not deal with out-of-state residents, and others block out certain states.

Other things to look for are a toll-free customer service number and automated customer assistance. You will want to check your credit balances often to make sure you are not going over your limit, and it is nice to be able to check twenty-four hours a day.

If you have an IRS lien or owe back taxes, some banks may not give you a secured credit card. If you have one of these problems, ask about their policy before sending any money.

Also ask about other rules: make sure the lender has a working phone number, a street address, income requirements, and no ongoing lawsuits. Sometimes it is possible to obtain an unsecured credit card, but these often require high up-front fees, offer a low credit line, and charge high interest rates.

It takes time to process paperwork for a post-bankruptcy secured or unsecured credit card. If you are in a hurry, you should start early. Most banks will not issue a card until you have received your discharge papers, but you can start talking with them before you actually have the papers in hand. Many will send out the application form prior to your receiving your discharge papers with the understanding that you must wait to send the application in until you receive the discharge. Most will want a copy of your discharge papers. You can speed the process up by sending a certified check or money order rather than a personal check.

Whether your secured card can be turned into an unsecured one will often depend on time—eighteen months, thirty-six months, or whatever. Also your FICO score will depend in part on how long you have been making timely payments on your debts. So it makes sense to get an early start.

Remember, your payment history only helps you if it is reported to a credit bureau—so ask if they report, and then after a few months order a copy of your credit report to be sure it is reported. You do not want to waste your time working with a bank that does not report to the credit bureaus.

Why should I even want a credit card?

You should think through why you are seeking a credit card. Is it a necessity? Making motel and airline reservations are often given as reasons why a person must have a credit card. Another reason is convenience. It is easier and safer to carry a credit card than a pocket full of cash. A third reason is to have a line of credit—a source of funds for an emergency.

It will be a while before you will have the use of a credit card for a real source of funds for an emergency. If you reaffirm a credit card debt, you will start off with a low credit line or no credit line at all. If you obtain a secured credit card, the credit limit will be so low it will not be much help.

Credit cards are convenient—perhaps too convenient. It is easy to whip out the plastic when you want to buy something without really thinking about the cost. That is what gets most of us in trouble. For day-to-day purchases, a card is not really better than carrying cash or debit cards and is inferior in one way. Most purchases such as dry cleaning, food, and gas are for relatively small amounts, less than $50 or $100. Carrying a few twenty dollar bills in your wallet would allow you to make these purchases. Credit cards are inferior to cash as using them is so easy, we often forget we made a purchase.

Opening your billfold or your purse psychologically makes you think about the purchase. You are more likely to elect to pass up the item, or at least remember you already spent money when you are considering another purchase. Credit cards are, of course, absolutely necessary for ordering items over the Internet or by phone. However, most items purchased over the Internet or from a mail order catalog are not necessities. Not buying these items is a good place to start to bring your spending under control.

For the next year or so, there is only one reason you want a credit card—to build a history of making your monthly payments on it in a timely way. Or to put it another way, to show the issuer that it will make money off of you. For this reason you will need to use your card for a few purchases, and not pay off the entire balance every month. People who pay off their entire balance each month do not pay any interest charges to the bank and thus the bank does not make any money off of them. They are known in the banking industry as "freeloaders" and some banks are instituting a monthly charge on people who never carry a balance from month to month.

> **Note:** The credit rating score (the FICO score) explanation is careful never to mention how important it is that they make money off of you and your credit cards through on-time payments—but we believe it is an important part of bank decisions on who to issue credit cards to.

Banks naturally prefer someone who will make them money over someone who is a freeloader. Think back to when you carried a large credit card debt over from month to month. You likely received many credit card applications in the mail and perhaps checks already made out to you ready to be cashed. You were an ideal customer, one who paid a minimum amount regularly each month, but who seldom paid off the entire balance, so the bank received those nice checks month after month like clockwork.

Your goal is to, in a small way, replicate that profile—running a balance each month, paying regularly in a timely way without having a large balance. Your real goal for the next few credit-rebuilding years is to have a few credit cards that carry a modest balance while you establish a record of paying on time each month. Do not worry about how a credit card is more convenient, or a source of emergency funds. You should very deliberately and carefully charge just enough each month to keep an ongoing balance. The balance should be low. Look at the Fair, Isaac chart—you want to have an outstanding balance of less than 15% of your available credit for a maximum score in that category.

Will department store credit cards help my credit score?

Another source of credit is department store cards. Department stores come in all sizes—from national chains to small one- or two-store operations. Often they will be more liberal in offering credit cards than the major credit card issuers. If you choose to try to obtain a department store card, be careful to investigate it beforehand. A request for credit may very well cause an inquiry on your credit report, so be sure to first try to get an idea if they will accept you and issue a card. In addition, make sure they will report your timely payments to the credit bureaus. You should look into department store credit cards, as having both a major credit card and department store cards picks up extra FICO points.

Will car loans help my credit score?

You can control the number of credit card applications you send out, but there are cases when you have less control over the number of inquiries that are made. If you should try to buy a car and obtain financing you are on dangerous ground. It is the custom among car dealers to take your financial information and shop your case among many lenders. This is known as *shot gunning*. The Fair, Isaac people say their formulas take shot gunning into account and compensate for it, so it does not hurt you.

When you are in the credit rebuilding stages and you need a vehicle, shop first for the financing and then the vehicle. The normal way people who do not have to worry about their credit shop for a car is to visit several car dealers and find a car they like. Then they ask about financing. Having fallen in love with one car, they are stuck with the dealer and its practices. The dealers may *shot gun* you.

What you should do is shop first for the financing, and after you have that nailed down, pick a car from what is available. One way to avoid too many inquiries is for you to obtain a copy of your credit report and show it to the financing manager early in your talks. You can then ask if he or she is likely to make a loan. You can also give him or her a copy of your FICO score. The financing manager will need to verify these later, but this is a good starting point. Tell the financing manager you are trying to avoid too many credit inquiries on your record.

Can I get a mortgage while rebuilding my credit?

Getting on track to buy a home can take longer than merely qualifying for a credit card. More money is at stake, so lenders are more careful. There are several different elements to consider.

First, the more money you can give as a down payment the easier, and sooner, it will be until you can qualify for a home loan. It will be hard for several years to qualify for a 5% down loan, easier to qualify for a 20% loan. Of course, this is of limited help if you have recently filed bankruptcy, because by definition you have very little extra money for a down payment. Another idea is to try to obtain an FHA loan. They often make loans with smaller down payments.

Owner financing is another possibility. In some cases, a seller will finance either the entire mortgage or a portion of the mortgage. Most sellers want a clean sale, but sometimes sellers who are having trouble selling their home or who for tax reasons are looking for a stream of monthly payments will consider this type of transaction. It does not hurt to ask.

Another possibility is a land contract or a lease with an option to buy. We suggest you stay away from this type of transaction as too many things can go wrong and cause you to lose your payments. If you use this option, make sure you have a lawyer draw up the papers.

Many people turn to *mortgage brokers* to find a loan. There are many good ones and just as many bad ones. Mortgage brokers are paid very well if the deal goes through and make nothing if the loan is not made. They are highly motivated to get the job done. Unfortunately, some will put you in subprime lending situations, often with balloon notes. We hear all the time of people who were told the deal would have one set of terms, and they set everything up to move into their new home after closing. Then they were presented with another set of terms at closing. Often they sign the new (worse) terms because they feel they have no option but to sign and move into the home. If you use a mortgage broker to find a loan, hire your own lawyer to review the proposed loan and to go to the closing with you.

Self-employed people have a harder time finding a loan, as they have irregular income. This makes lenders uneasy. Having a harder time buying a home is one of the prices you pay for being your own boss. If you are self-employed and really want to speed up rebuilding your credit, it is far easier and maybe wiser to obtain a job with a steady income. You miss the highs and independence but gain the steady cash flow. If you do not want to work for someone else, or cannot find the right job, then it is best to not try to push the credit rebuilding process.

Can I travel without credit?

While rebuilding their credit, people often worry about their ability to travel. Most motels and hotels are set up to have you guarantee your reservation with a credit card. We advise our clients who travel to simply use their debit card to make reservations. They are accepted as broadly as credit cards and normally are not charged until you arrive.

Glossary

A

accelerate. When a debtor fails to meet a requirement of the loan (such as making timely payments) and the creditor calls for the entire loan balance to be paid at once.

automatic stay. An order issued by the bankruptcy court stopping collection action against the person or business that filed bankruptcy.

B

balloon mortgage. A mortgage that offers lower payments for a set period of time, then demands the remainder of the debt be repayed (with interest) in a lump sum.

bankruptcy estate. The sum of the property and assets owned by the person or business who filed bankruptcy.

bankruptcy trustee. A person appointed by the court to protect the rights of creditors of the bankruptcy filer.

bar date. Date after which creditors may not raise objections to the discharge of their debt following a sixty-day period of suspense.

C

Chapter 7. A type of bankruptcy filed by either a corporation or an individual. It provides for the cancellation of certain unsecured debts without a repayment plan and may, but often does not, call for the sale of some of the filer's assets.

Chapter 11. A type of bankruptcy filed by either a corporation or an individual (but normally a corporation). It provides for the reorganization of the debts of the filer and provides for a plan of repayment of debts in whole or part.

Chapter 12. A type of bankruptcy for family farms.

Chapter 13. A type of bankruptcy filing for individuals with regular income. It provides for the repayment, in whole or part, of the individual's debts through regular payments to a Chapter 13 trustee over a period of three to five years.

civil lawsuit. A lawsuit against a person or entity that does not carry a criminal penalty. Lawsuits to collect debts by individuals or entities are almost always civil rather than criminal and therefore a debtor is not in danger of going to jail.

collateral. Property that is promised by a borrower as security for a loan. (See *lien*).

committee of creditors. Small groups that represent the creditors in general.

contingent debt. A debt that you may have to pay if an agreed upon event takes place.

corporation. A type of legal entity set up under state law that is treated for many purposes as a separate person.

cosigned debt. Debt carried by two or more parties simultaneously; typically occurs when one party has insufficient credit to secure a loan on their own–if said party is unable to make payments, the second party will be liable for the entire debt and must take up the payments or suffer equal consequences to their credit.

creditor. A person or business that has money owed to it.

credit rating. A score that states a person's or business's creditworthiness. It is often used in deciding whether or not to make a loan.

credit report. A report produced by a credit bureau showing a person's or business's debts and repayment history.

D

debt. A promise to pay someone a sum of money. (See *contingent debt* and *secured debt*.)

debtor. A person or business that owes money to another.

debtor in possession. Business owners or management that continue to run the business during a Chapter 11 proceeding.

debt to income ratio. A number computed by dividing your income by your debt.

default. The failure by a debtor to act as required in a loan contract. This is normally a failure to make payments on a debt when due.

deficiency. In a repossession, the difference between a loan amount for a property and what is received for the property at auction.

disposable income test. A test that requires all disposable income be devoted to the Chapter 13 plan in order for a judge to approve your Chapter 13 bankruptcy.

disclosure statement. A summary of the plan of reorganization and how different types of creditors will be treated in a Chapter 11 bankruptcy. The statement includes an overview of the finances of the filing entity and an assessment of what would happen if other alternatives were followed.

disputed debt. A debt a third party claims you owe him or her, but which you deny.

E

Employee Retirement Income Security Act (ERISA). A 1970s-era law that aims to protect employee retirement funds. It sets conditions that sponsors (normally employers) must meet to claim tax benefits for contributions to a retirement or other benefit program.

equity value. The difference between the market value of a house and what is owed on it in first, second, and third mortgages.

exempt property. Property a debtor is allowed to keep while in bankruptcy.

F

522 limitation. A limitation on the amount a debtor can exempt a residence or homestead if that property was acquired by the debtor during the 1,215 days prior to filing bankruptcy.

foreclosure. A legal process whereby a lien holder (mortgage holder) moves to take land and any buildings on it.

freeze. A financial action that takes place when a person or entity holding funds refuses to release those funds because of a breach by the owner of the funds. For example, when a debtor fails to pay a loan to a bank, the bank may hold on to money in the debtor's savings account.

G

garnish. A collecting tool that removes money from your paycheck to send directly to creditors.

H

hardship withdrawal. The right to withdraw funds from tax qualified pension or retirement savings when an unexpected emergency occurs or there is a pressing need for the funds.

home equity loan. A loan secured by an interest in the borrower's home. It creates a mortgage against the home.

I

IRS living expenses. Established national standards for necessary expenses.

J

judgment. An order of a court. If the order states that money is owed, it is a money judgment.

judgment lien. A money judgment that attaches against property. The judgment lien must be paid when the home is sold or refinanced. It is possible in some cases to remove a judgment lien in a bankruptcy.

judgment proof. A person or business that has no assets a creditor can reach to collect court-awarded judgments. In most states, a debtor may protect a certain amount of assets despite the fact that a creditor has a judgment against the debtor. If the debtor's assets are within the protected limits, the creditor may not collect on the judgment.

L

lead time. A period of time in advance of an expected action or event. It is normally used to prepare the expected action or event or to perform an action.

leasor. An individual or entity that allows the use of property in exchange for periodic payments. Most commonly a person or entity allowing use of a vehicle or an apartment in exchange for monthly payments.

lien. A claim by a creditor against property of the debtor to insure that a debt is paid. Common examples of liens are loans secured by a claim against a vehicle and mortgages on homes.

liquidate. To sell all assets.

M

market value. The price at which a person could sell his or her home.

means test. A mathematical calculation to determine whether the petitioner must file a Chapter 13 or a Chapter 7 bankruptcy. If the filer is above the state's median family income, he or she will have to pass this test or be forced to file a Chapter 13.

meeting of creditors (341 meeting). A bankruptcy hearing where creditors and the trustee are allowed to question a bankruptcy filer about his financial affairs.

money judgment. A court order directing the payment of money.

mortgage. A lien or claim against real property given to a creditor. The most common usage is a claim against one's home in exchange for the lending of money.

N
net pay. The amount of money a person has each month after deducting taxes, insurance, and retirement funds from his or her paycheck.

O
operating costs. For transportation, the costs necessary for a vehicle to function, such as gas, inspections, oil changes, and repairs.

P
personal guarantee. A promise by a person or business to pay a debt that is not backed by a security interest. Often it is a promise to pay a debt if another person does not pay it. It makes the person giving the guarantee fully responsible for any portion of the debt that is not paid to the lender.

petitioner. A person or corporation that has filed bankruptcy.

plan. In bankruptcy, it is the written description filed by an individual or a corporation describing how debts will be treated. Bankruptcy plans are used in Chapter 11 and Chapter 13 bankruptcy filings.

process server. One who delivers lawsuit papers. Can be law enforcement personnel or an authorized private individual. The term normally refers to a private individual.

property. An item that has value. It can be land, accounts receivable, investments, household or business goods, vehicles, land, etc.

prorate. A method of sharing funds among several people or entities according to a set criteria.

Q

quick ratio. As used in this book, it is the total of unsecured debts divided by one year's disposable income. In financial analysis, it is cash, marketable securities, and accounts receivable divided by current liabilities.

R

reaffirmation agreement. Agreement signed by a bankruptcy petitioner stating he will continue paying a given debt owed to a creditor after the bankruptcy is completed. This is normally done for one of three reasons: a sense of moral obligation; to keep access to credit offered by a creditor (as in credit cards); or to keep collateral such as a vehicle that is subject to repossession.

real estate. Land with or without buildings on it (also called real property).

repossession. The taking of property that has been pledged as security or collateral for the repayment of a loan. A repossession can be done with or without a court order.

right of offset. The ability of a person or business that holds another's money (like a bank) to apply the money being held to a debt that is owed to that person or business. For example, a bank can apply money from your account to an overdrawn check on your account.

S

section 341 meeting. A chance for creditors to ask questions during a Chapter 7 filing.

secured creditor. An entity with legal rights to take back ownership of a property if a debtor fails to repay the loan on the property.

secured debt. A debt that is backed or secured by a claim on property. Examples are mortgages or claims against vehicles.

security/secured goods. Property and dollar limits a person can keep despite filing for bankruptcy. (See *collateral*.)

security interest. The claim or lien on an item of property or an asset created by an agreement between a debtor and a creditor. This is different from a judgment lien or a tax lien created by a court or action of law.

senior lien. An item of property may have more than one claim against it. The senior lien is the one that must be paid or satisfied first. An example is a first mortgage where there is a first and second mortgage.

service of lawsuit papers. The delivery of a complaint or other lawsuit papers. This starts a lawsuit against the defendant. Lawsuit papers can be served by certified mail, a sheriff, or other legal officer, or by a process server.

standing line of credit. An agreement between a financial institution and an individual that establishes a maximum loan balance.

statement of intentions. A declaration in a bankruptcy petition stating how secured and other debts will be treated.

statutory lien. A claim created by a statute or operation of the law. A common example is a tax lien against property.

stockholder. One who owns an interest in a corporation.

subprime loan or mortgage. A loan or mortgage to a person whose credit record or standing causes him or her to need to pay a higher interest rate or who would normally be turned down when asking for a loan or mortgage.

T

tax lien. A claim by a tax authority against property because of an overdue tax debt or obligation.

trustee. A person or entity that has a claim on property for the benefit of a third party. Common examples are a trustee in connection with a home mortgage or a bankruptcy trustee. In bankruptcy, the term is used to refer to the bankruptcy trustee.

U

unmatured debt. Debt in which the event creating the duty to pay has not yet occurred.

unsecured debt. A debt not secured by an interest in an item of property or an asset.

unsecured loan. A promise by an individual or entity to pay a debt that is not backed by a security interest.

W

wage earner plan (or wage earner bankruptcy). Another name for a Chapter 13 bankruptcy.

wage garnishment. The taking of all or part of a debtor's wages for the benefit of a creditor. The employer takes the wages earned by the debtor and sends it to the creditor. This is done for private non-governmental creditors only after a money judgment. Government creditors can have a wage garnishment put in place without a court order.

wild card (or wild card exemption). The right to protect from creditors or a bankruptcy trustee any item of property up to a set dollar value.

workout (or workout program). An arrangement to pay a debt after the debt has gone into default.

Appendix A

FEDERAL AND STATE-SPECIFIC BANKRUPTCY EXEMPTIONS

Throughout the text of this book, there are several references to various exemptions one can take in bankruptcy. These are dollar amounts and limits on certain items (i.e., your home, vehicles, etc.) that cannot be used to pay your creditors. Listed in this appendix are both federal exemptions and any state-specific ones. Refer to your state below; there is a list of states that allow your choice of federal or your state's exemptions.

The bankruptcy exemption law was changed in 2005 to provide for a look back to control what exemption laws are used when people move between states shortly before filing bankruptcy. If you have lived in the state in which you file for less than 730 days, you must look back and use your prior state's exemption.

Working out which state's exemptions are used is complex. You count the 180 days before the 730-day period and work out what state you were domiciled in for the majority of that 180-day period. That state's exemptions are used.

There are problems with the 180-day counting program set up by Congress. Sometimes a debtor is not domiciled in any state (he or she has been traveling, etc.) or the prior state will only allow residents of that state to use its exemptions. In those cases the debtor would use the federal exemptions. If you fall into the 730-day look back rule, you should see a lawyer.

The following is not intended to provide legal advice but to only provide general guidelines. A lawyer should be seen to learn the exact exemptions in each state and how they operate in a given case.

FEDERAL BANKRUPTCY EXEMPTIONS

Homestead up to:	$20,200
Motor Vehicle up to:	$3,225
Personal Property up to:	$525 of value per item; $10,775 total
Tools of Trade up to:	$2,205
Jewelry up to:	$1,350
Wild Card:	$1,075 plus up to $10,125 of any unused amount of the homestead exemption

Please note that the dollar amounts will change every year.

Federal exemptions can be used as an alternate to state exemptions by residents of the following states and the District of Columbia.

Alaska
Arkansas
Connecticut
District of Columbia
Hawaii
Kentucky
Massachusetts
Michigan
Minnesota

New Hampshire
New Jersey
New Mexico
Pennsylvania
Rhode Island
Texas
Vermont
Washington
Wisconsin

STATE EXEMPTIONS

Alabama

Homestead up to:	$5,000 (160 acres maximum)
Motor Vehicle:	Vehicle for business
Personal Property up to:	All household goods, apparel, books
Tools of Trade:	Military equipment Necessary tools
Wild Card:	$3,000

Alaska

Homestead up to:	$67,500
Motor Vehicle up to:	$3,750 (if value of the vehicle is not over $25,000)
Personal Property up to:	$3,000
Tools of Trade up to:	$2,800, but counts against personal property limit
Jewelry up to:	$1,250, but counts against personal property limit

Arizona

Homestead up to:	$150,000 Limited to $136,875 if property acquired within 1,215 days of filing for bankruptcy
Motor Vehicle up to:	$5,000 ($10,000 if physically disabled)

Personal Property up to:	$4,000 household furnishings $500 clothing $250 personal library $500 pets
Tools of Trade up to:	$2,500
Jewelry up to:	$1,000 wedding and engagement rings

Arkansas

Homestead up to:	Unlimited if property under ¼ (.25) acre in the city or 80 acres elsewhere $2,500 if between ¼ (.25) and 1 acre in the city, or 80–160 acres elsewhere
Motor Vehicle up to:	None
Personal Property up to:	$200 if single or $500 if married No limit on the value of clothing
Tools of Trade:	None

California

Note: There are two options for bankruptcy exemptions in California. The two systems cannot be mixed.

Option 1

Homestead up to:	$50,000 if single $75,000 if a member of a family and no one else is claiming a homestead $150,000 if 65 or older or disabled; if you are single, 55 or older, and earn less than $15,000 per year; or if you are married, 55 or older, and earn less than $20,000

Motor Vehicle up to:	$2,550
Personal Property up to:	All food, clothing, appliances, furnishings, and health aids $2,700 home building materials
Tools of Trade up to:	$6,750
Jewelry up to:	$6,750

Option 2

Homestead up to:	$20,725
Motor Vehicle up to:	$3,300
Personal Property up to:	Clothing, household goods, appliances, furnishings, animals, books, musical instruments, and crops—$525 per item
Tools of Trade up to:	$2,075
Jewelry up to:	$1,350
Wild Card:	$1,100 and any unused portion of the homestead exemption can be used to protect personal property

Colorado

Homestead up to:	$60,000 (property must be occupied at the time of filing) $90,000 if elderly or disabled
Motor Vehicle up to:	$5,000 or $10,000 if elderly or disabled
Personal Property up to:	$3,000 household goods $1,500 clothing $1,500 books and pictures $600 food and fuel Health aids

Tools of Trade up to:	$20,000 $3,000 library of a professional $50,000 farm materials and animals for a farmer
Jewelry up to:	$2,000

Connecticut

Homestead up to:	$75,000
Motor Vehicle up to:	$3,500
Personal Property:	Food, clothing, health aids, appliances, furniture, bedding
Tools of Trade:	All needed tools and books, instruments, military equipment, and farm animals
Jewelry:	Wedding and engagement rings
Wild Card:	$1,000 of any property

Delaware

Homestead up to:	$50,000
Motor Vehicle up to:	$15,000 (any amount not used can be applied to tools of trade)
Personal Property:	$500 per person—clothing, jewelry, books, family pictures, piano, school books, and family library
Tools of Trade up to:	$15,000 minus the amount used for motor vehicle

Note: Total exemption for personal property may not exceed $25,000 per person

District of Columbia

Homestead up to:	Unlimited so long as it is used as debtor's residence Limited to $136,875 if property acquired within 1,215 days of filing for bankruptcy
Motor Vehicle up to:	$2,575
Personal Property up to:	$425 per item; $8,625 total $400 family pictures and library
Tools of Trade up to:	$1,625

Note: These exemptions can be claimed by residents of D.C. or by those who earn the major part of their income in D.C.

Florida

Homestead up to:	Unlimited if property under ½ (.5) acre in the city or 160 acres elsewhere Limited to $136,875 if property acquired within 1,215 days of filing for bankruptcy
Motor Vehicle up to:	$1,000
Personal Property up to:	$1,000 Health aids
Tools of Trade:	Included in personal property

Georgia

Homestead up to:	$10,000
Motor Vehicle up to:	$3,500
Personal Property up to:	$300 per household item; $5,000 total
Tools of Trade up to:	$1,500
Jewelry up to:	$500
Wild Card:	$600 to protect any property $5,600 of unused homestead exemption

Hawaii

Homestead up to:	$20,000 or $30,000 for head of family or over 65
Motor Vehicle up to:	$2,575
Personal Property:	All necessary household goods
Tools of Trade:	All tools needed for livelihood (can include car and commercial fishing boat)
Jewelry up to:	$1,000

Note: Property cannot exceed 1 acre for Homestead exemption

Idaho

Homestead up to:	$100,000
Motor Vehicle up to:	$3,000
Personal Property up to:	$500 per household good; $5,000 total $500 per item of apparel; $5,000 total
Tools of Trade up to:	$1,500 All arms and equipment kept by peace officers and military personnel
Jewelry up to:	$1,000

Illinois

Homestead up to:	$15,000
Motor Vehicle up to:	$2,400
Personal Property up to:	$4,000, plus needed clothes, health aids, school books and bibles
Tools of Trade up to:	$1,500

Indiana

Homestead up to:	$15,000
Motor Vehicle:	Included in personal property
Personal Property up to:	$8,000 real estate or tangible property $300 intangible personal property
Tools of Trade:	National Guard uniforms and equipment

Iowa

Homestead up to:	Unlimited if property under ½ (.5) acre in town or 40 acres elsewhere Limited to $136,875 if property acquired within 1,215 days of filing for bankruptcy
Motor Vehicles up to:	$7,000
Personal Property up to:	$7,000 clothing, household goods $1,000 personal library
Tools of Trade up to:	$10,000 non-farming equipment $10,000 farming equipment and livestock
Jewelry up to:	$2,000 plus exemption for wedding rings

Kansas

Homestead up to:	Unlimited if property under 1 acre in town or 160 acres elsewhere Limited to $136,875 if property acquired within 1,215 days of filing for bankruptcy
Motor Vehicle up to:	$20,000 or Unlimited if designed for disabled person
Personal Property up to:	All household goods, food, fuel, and clothing to last one year
Tools of Trade up to:	$7,500 National Guard uniforms and equipment
Jewelry up to:	$1,000

Kentucky

Homestead up to:	$5,000
Motor Vehicle up to:	$2,500
Personal Property up to:	$3,000 household goods including jewelry
Tools of Trade up to:	$3,000 farm equipment and livestock $300 nonfarming tools $2,500 vehicle for a mechanic or electrical equipment servicer $1,000 library and office equipment
Wild Card:	$1,000

Louisiana

Homestead up to:	$25,000; limited to 5 acres in city or 200 acres elsewhere
Motor Vehicle up to:	$7,500
Personal Property:	Unlimited
Tools of Trade:	Tools, books, instruments, a vehicle, and a utility trailer needed for work
Jewelry up to:	$5,000 wedding and engagement rings

Maine

Homestead up to:	$47,500 $95,000 if caring for dependents $95,000 if age 60 or older or disabled
Motor Vehicle up to:	$5,000
Personal Property up to:	Health aids $200 per item of personal property $400 any property
Tools of Trade up to:	$5,000
Jewelry up to:	$750

Maryland

Homestead up to:	$5,000
Motor Vehicle:	None (can use wild card)
Personal Property up to:	$1,000 clothing, household goods, pets
Tools of Trade up to:	$5,000
Wild Card:	$6,000

Massachusetts

Homestead up to:	$500,000 Limited to $136,875 if property acquired within 1,215 days of filing for bankruptcy
Motor Vehicle up to:	$700
Personal Property up to:	Necessary clothes and bedding $3,000 furniture $200 books $200 per month for rent (if no homestead exemption used) $300 food, farm animals, and hay
Tools of Trade up to:	$500 plus $500 materials you designed $500 boat and fisherman's equipment

Michigan

Homestead up to:	$34,450 $51,650 if disabled or age 65 or older
Motor Vehicle up to:	$3,175
Personal Property up to:	$525 per item; $3,450 total All necessary clothing
Tools of Trade up to:	$2,300

Minnesota

Homestead up to:	$300,000 or $750,000 if primarily used for agriculture; under ½ (.5) acre in town or 160 acres elsewhere Unlimited for manufactured homes Limited to $136,875 if property acquired within 1,215 days of filing for bankruptcy
Motor Vehicle up to:	$4,200 $42,000 for vehicle modified to serve a disabled person
Personal Property:	$9,450
Tools of Trade:	$10,500 $13,000 farm implements
Jewelry up to:	$2,572 wedding rings

Note: Except for homestead, all exemptions were set in 1972 dollars and expected to grow with inflation

Mississippi

Homestead up to:	$75,000; limited to 160 acres $30,000 manufactured housing
Motor Vehicle:	Included under personal property
Personal Property up to:	$10,000 $50,000 if over age 70
Tools of Trade:	Included under personal property

Missouri

Homestead up to:	$15,000 $5,000 mobile home
Motor Vehicles up to:	$3,000
Personal Property up to:	$3,000 personal goods Health aids
Tools of Trade up to:	$3,000
Jewelry up to:	$500 $1,500 wedding ring
Wild Card:	$600

Montana

Homestead up to:	$250,000 Limited to $136,875 if property acquired within 1,215 days of filing for bankruptcy
Motor Vehicle up to:	$2,500
Personal Property up to:	$600 per item; $4,500 total Health aids
Tools of Trade up to:	$3,000

Nebraska

Homestead up to:	$60,000; no more than 2 contiguous lots in a city or 160 acres elsewhere
Motor Vehicle:	Included under personal property
Personal Property up to:	$1,500 Health aids
Tools of Trade up to:	$2,400 May include one vehicle if used for principal business or commute to same
Wild Card:	$2,500 to protect any property if homestead exemption is not used

Nevada

Homestead up to:	$550,000 Limited to $136,875 if property acquired within 1,215 days of filing for bankruptcy
Motor Vehicle up to:	$15,000 Unlimited if equipped for the disabled
Personal Property up to:	$12,000 household goods $5,000 books and jewelry Health aids $1,000 in any personal property
Tools of Trade up to:	$10,000 $4,500 farm equipment $4,500 mining equipment All military equipment
Wild Card:	$1,000

New Hampshire

Homestead up to:	$100,000
Motor Vehicle up to:	$4,000
Personal Property up to:	$3,500 furniture, household goods $800 books Necessary clothes Farm animals and hay
Tools of Trade up to:	$5,000 All military equipment Listed barnyard animals or a yoke of oxen when needed for farming
Jewelry up to:	$500
Wild Card:	$1,000 plus $7,000 of any unused exemptions

New Jersey

Homestead:	None
Motor Vehicle:	Included under personal property
Personal Property up to:	$1,000 personal property $1,000 household goods Clothing
Tools of Trade:	None

New Mexico

Homestead up to:	$60,000
Motor Vehicle up to:	$4,000
Personal Property up to:	$500 plus All household goods
Tools of Trade up to:	$1,500
Jewelry up to:	$2,500
Wild Card:	$5,000 if homestead not claimed

New York

Homestead up to:	$50,000
Motor Vehicle up to:	$2,400
Personal Property up to:	$50 books $35 watch $450 food for domestic animals Most household goods
Tools of Trade up to:	$600
Wild Card:	$2,500 cash in lieu of homestead and personal property exemptions

North Carolina

Homestead up to:	$18,500 $37,000 for widow/widower over 65
Motor Vehicle up to:	$3,500
Personal Property up to:	$5,000 plus $1,000 per dependent (up to $4,000)
Tools of Trade up to:	$2,000
Wild Card:	$5,000 of unused homestead exemption can be used to protect other property

North Dakota

Homestead up to:	$80,000
Motor Vehicle up to:	$1,200 $32,000 if modified for a disabled owner
Personal Property up to:	Clothing, $100 books, pictures, 1 year fuel Crops/grains raised on debtor's land Head of family (if not claiming crops) may claim: $5,000 property, or $1,000 furniture, $1,500 books, $1,000 tools of the trade, and $4,500 farm implements and livestock A single person may claim $2,500 property
Tools of Trade:	Included under personal property
Wild Card:	$7,500 if homestead exemption not used

Ohio

Homestead up to:	$20,200
Motor Vehicle up to:	$3,225
Personal Property up to:	$525 per item household goods, furnishings, books, animals, firearms, crops; $10,775 total Health aids $1,075 any personal property $400 cash
Tools of Trade up to:	$2,025
Jewelry up to:	$1,350

Oklahoma

Homestead up to:	Unlimited if property under 1 acre in city or 160 acres elsewhere $5,000 if homestead is in city and used for both business and residence, and the residence is at least 75% of property Limited to $136,875 if property acquired within 1,215 days of filing for bankruptcy
Motor Vehicles up to:	$7,500
Personal Property up to:	$4,000 clothes All furniture, books, pictures, health aids 1 year of food 2 bridles, 2 saddles, 100 chickens, 20 sheep, 10 hogs, 5 cows, 2 horses, and forage for livestock to last 1 year
Tools of Trade up to:	$10,000 $2,000 guns
Jewelry up to:	$3,000 wedding and anniversary rings

Oregon

Homestead up to:	$30,000 land you own ($39,600 if jointly owned) $23,000 mobile home on land you own ($30,000 if jointly owned) $20,000 mobile home on land you don't own ($30,000 if jointly owned)
Motor Vehicle up to:	$2,150
Personal Property up to:	$1,800 clothes, jewelry, personal items $3,000 household items, furniture $600 books, pictures, instruments $1,000 domestic animals and poultry All health aids $400 any personal property not already covered under another exemption
Tools of Trade up to:	$3,000

Pennsylvania

Homestead:	None
Motor Vehicle:	Included under personal property
Personal Property up to:	$300 any property Clothes, bibles, school books, uniforms
Tools of Trade:	None

Rhode Island

Homestead up to:	$300,000 Limited to $136,875 if property acquired within 1,215 days of filing for bankruptcy
Motor Vehicle up to:	$12,000
Personal Property up to:	$9,600 household goods and furniture $300 books Clothing
Tools of Trade up to:	$1,500 Practicing professional's library
Jewelry up to:	$2,000
Wild Card:	$5,000

South Carolina

Homestead up to:	$51,450
Motor Vehicle up to:	$5,150
Personal Property up to:	$4,125
Tools of Trade up to:	$1,550
Jewelry up to:	$1,025
Wild Card:	$5,150 if homestead exemption not claimed

South Dakota

Homestead up to:	Unlimited if property under 1 acre in town or 160 acres elsewhere Unlimited for mobile homes Limited to $136,875 if property acquired within 1,215 days of filing for bankruptcy
Motor Vehicle:	Included under personal property
Personal Property up to:	$6,000 for head of family $4,000 if single $200 books Clothing
Tools of Trade:	Included under personal property

Tennessee

Homestead up to:	$5,000 for single $7,500 for married couple $12,000 for single over age 62 $20,000 for married couple where one person is over age 62 $25,000 for married couple where both partners are over age 62 or for single who with custody of 1 or more minors
Motor Vehicle:	Included under personal property
Personal Property up to:	$4,000 Clothes, school books, pictures, bibles
Tools of Trade up to:	$1,900

Texas

Homestead up to:	Unlimited if property under 10 acres in town or 100 acres elsewhere (200 acres for family) Limited to $136,875 if property acquired within 1,215 days of filing for bankruptcy
Motor Vehicle up to:	One motor vehicle *See limitation under personal property*
Personal Property up to:	Home furnishings, food, clothes 2 firearms, sports equipment, 2 horses or mules with riding equipment, 12 cattle, 60 other livestock, 120 fowl, feed for the animals and household pets $30,000 limit for total value of vehicles, personal property, owed wages, and tools of trade ($60,000 limit for head of family)
Tools of Trade:	Tools, books, equipment, including motor vehicles, boats, farming/ranch vehicles, and instruments used in a trade/profession *See limitation under personal property*
Jewelry up to:	Up to 25% of aggregate value of personal property exemption *See limitation under personal property*

Utah

Homestead up to:	$20,000 if primary residence $5,000 if not primary residence
Motor Vehicle up to:	$2,500
Personal Property up to:	All clothing except jewelry and furs Refrigerator, freezer, stove, washer, dryer, sewing machine, health aids, 1 year of food, bedding $500 sofas, chairs, related furnishings $500 dining and kitchen tables and chairs $500 animals, books, musical instruments $500 heirlooms, item of sentimental value
Tools of Trade up to:	$3,500 business tools, books, implements National Guard uniforms and equipment

Vermont

Homestead up to:	$75,000
Motor Vehicle up to:	$2,500
Personal Property up to:	$2,500 clothes, goods, furnishings, appliances, books, animals, and crops $5,000 growing crops
Tools of Trade up to:	$5,000
Jewelry up to:	$500 plus wedding rings
Wild Card:	$400 any property plus up to $7,000 unused exemptions

Virginia

Homestead up to:	$5,000 plus $500 per dependent
Motor Vehicle up to:	$2,000
Personal Property up to:	$1,000 clothing $5,000 household furnishings $5,000 heirlooms Health aids
Tools of Trade up to:	$10,000 tools, books, instruments, equipment, and machines necessary for use in occupation or trade Farmer: $3,000 tractor, 1 wagon or cart, pair of horses, $1,000 fertilizer, 2 plows Military arms, uniforms, and equipment
Jewelry:	Wedding and engagement rings
Wild Card:	$2,000 for 40% or more disabled veterans with a service-related disability

Washington

Homestead up to:	$125,000
Motor Vehicle up to:	$2,500
Personal Property up to:	$1,000 clothing and jewelry $2,700 household goods $1,500 books and private libraries $2,000 any property (no more than $200 cash, stocks, or bonds)
Tools of Trade up to:	$5,000

West Virginia

Homestead up to:	$25,000
Motor Vehicle up to:	$2,400
Personal Property up to:	$400 per item; $8,000 total
Tools of Trade up to:	$1,500
Jewelry up to:	$1,000
Wild Card:	$800 plus any unused portion of homestead exemption

Wisconsin

Homestead up to:	$40,000
Motor Vehicle up to:	$1,200 plus any unused personal property exemption
Personal Property up to:	$5,000 household goods, including jewelry, sporting goods, and animals $1,000 in deposit accounts
Tools of Trade up to:	$7,500

Wyoming

Homestead up to:	$10,000 $6,000 mobile home
Motor Vehicle up to:	$2,400
Personal Property up to:	$1,000 clothing and wedding rings $2,000 household items School books, pictures, bibles
Tools of Trade up to:	$2,000

Appendix B

CONSUMER CREDIT COUNSELING SERVICES

The following agencies are accredited members of the National Foundation for Credit Counseling.

National Foundation for Credit Counseling
801 Roeder Rd., Suite 900
Silver Spring, MD 20910
(301) 589–5600
(800) 388–2227
www.nfcc.org

LOCAL CONSUMER CREDIT COUNSELING SERVICES

Alabama

CCCS of Alabama, Inc.
www.budgethelp.com
(800) 662–6119

Andalusia Branch
300 E. Three Notch St.
Andalusia, AL 36420

Montgomery Branch
777 S. Lawrence St., Suite 101
Montgomery, AL 36104

Dothan Branch
175 Belmont Dr., Suite 1
Dothan, AL 36305

Selma Branch
116 Mabry St.
Selma, AL 36701

Enterprise Branch
116 S. Main St., Suite 310
Enterprise, AL 36330

Tuscaloosa Branch
2316 University Blvd.
Tuscaloosa, AL 35401

Family Counseling Center of Mobile, Inc.
www.cccsmobile.org
(251) 602–0011
(888) 880–1416

CCCS of Jackson
208 Commerce St.
Jackson, AL 36545

CCCS of Montrose
22787 Highway 98, Bldg. B-2
Montrose, AL 36559

CCCS of Mobile
705 E. Oak Circle Dr.
Mobile, AL 36609

Gateway Family & Child Services
www.gway.org
(205) 251–1572
(888) 260–2227

Birmingham Branch
1401 S. 20th St., Suite 100
Birmingham, AL 35205

CCCS of the Tennessee River Valley
www.mycreditcounselors.com
(256) 881–1000

Huntsville Branch
1015 Airport Rd.
Huntsville, AL 35802

CCCS of West Florida
(251) 694–1458
(866) 393–1233

Mobile Branch
3250 Airport Blvd. F-1
Mobile, AL 36606

Alaska

CCCS of Alaska
www.cccsofak.com
(800) 478–6501

Anchorage Branch
208 E. 4th Ave.
Anchorage, AK 99501

Fairbanks Branch
250 Cushman St., Suite 4B
Fairbanks, AK 99701

Arizona

Money Management International
www.moneymanagement.org
(866) 889–9347

Flagstaff Branch
2615 N. 4th St., Suite 2
Flagstaff, AZ 86004

Mesa Branch
1234 S. Power Rd., Suite 100
Mesa, AZ 85206

Glendale Branch
17235 N. 75th Ave.,
Suite C-125
Glendale, AZ 85308

Phoenix (Central) Branch
722 E. Osborn Rd., Suite 210
Phoenix, AZ 85014

Phoenix (North) Branch
1717 E. Bell Rd., Suite 7
Phoenix, AZ 85308

Prescott Branch
1215 Gail Gardener Way, Suite B
Prescott, AZ 86305

Tempe Branch
950 W. Elliot Rd., Suite 122
Tempe, AZ 85284

Tucson (East) Branch
5515 E. Grant Rd., Suite 211
Tucson, AZ 85712

Tucson (West) Branch
4732 N. Oracle Rd., Suite 217
Tucson, AZ 85705

Yuma Branch
2450 S. Fourth Ave., Suite 500
Yuma, AZ 85364

GreenPath Debt Solutions
www.greenpath.com
(866) 648–8114

Tempe Branch
401 W. Baseline, Suite 206
Tempe, AZ 85283

Arkansas

Credit Counseling of Arkansas, Inc.
www.ccoacares.com
(479) 521–8877
(800) 889–4916

Bentonville Branch
1740 Moberly Ln., Suite A
Bentonville, AR 72712

Fayetteville Branch
1111 E. Zion Rd.
Fayetteville, AR 72703

Fort Smith Branch
2301 S. 56th St., Suite 103
Fort Smith, AR 72903

Harrison Branch
128 W. Stephenson St.
Harrison, AR 72601

Siloam Springs Branch
151 Highway 412 E, Suite G
Siloam Springs, AR 72761

Springdale Branch
614 E. Emma
Springdale, AR 72764

Family Service Agency
www.helpingfamilies.org
(501) 753–0202
(800) 255–2227

Conway Branch
740 S. Salem Rd., Suite 104
Conway, AR 72032

Little Rock Branch
300 S. Rodney Parham, Suite 6
Little Rock, AR 72205

Fort Smith Branch
5111 Rogers Ave., Suite 553
Fort Smith, AR 72903

North Little Rock Branch
628 W. Broadway, Suite 203
North Little Rock, AR 72114

Hot Springs Branch
1401 Malvern Ave., Suite 100
Hot Springs, AR 71913

Pine Bluff Branch
211 W. 3rd, Suite 215
Pine Bluff, AR 71601

Jacksonville Branch
Arkansas Federal Credit Union Bldg.
2424 Marshall Rd.
Jacksonville, AR 72076

Russellville Branch
Bank of the Ozarks
2305 E. Pkwy.
Russellville, AR 72802

Money Management International
www.moneymanagement.org
(866) 889–9347

El Dorado Branch
202 N. Washington, Suite 101
El Dorado, AR 71730

ClearPoint Financial Solutions, Inc.
www.clearpointcreditcounselingsolutions.org
(877) 422–9040

Jonesboro Branch
2218 E. Race St.
Jonesboro, AR 72401

CCCS of Springfield/Joplin/West Plains
www.cccsoftheozarks.org
(800) 346–4934

Mountain Home Branch
US Bank Bldg.
100 S. Main
Mountain Home, AR 72653

California

ByDesign Financial Solutions
www.bydesignsolutions.org
(323) 890–9500
(800) 750–2227

Los Angeles
Glendale Branch
412 W. Broadway, Suite 212
Glendale, CA 91204

Granada Hills Branch
16800 Devonshire, #301
Granada Hills, CA 91344

Los Angeles Branch
6001 E. Washington Blvd., Suite 200
Los Angeles, CA 90040

Palmdale/Lancaster Branch
1605 E. Palmdale Blvd., #E
Palmdale, CA 93550

San Bernardino Branch
242 E. Airport Dr., Suite 107
San Bernardino, CA 92408

Sacramento Valley
Sacramento Branch
4636 Watt Ave., 2nd Floor
North Highlands, CA 95660

Redding Branch
1260 Pine St.
Redding, CA 96001

Central Valley
Fresno Branch
4969 E. McKinley Ave., #107
Fresno, CA 93727

Mid-Counties
Merced Branch
3351 M St.
Merced, CA 95348

Modesto Branch
1101 Standiford Plaza, Suite D-4
Modesto, CA 95350

Stockton Branch
2291 W. March Ln., Suite A110
Stockton, CA 95207

Money Management International
www.moneymanagement.org
(866) 889–9347

Berkeley Branch
2140 Shattuck Ave., Suite 1208
Berkeley, CA 94704

Oakland Branch
7677 Oakport St., Suite 700
Oakland, CA 94621

Chula Vista Branch
Pacific Western Bank
730 Broadway, Suite 200
Chula Vista, CA 91911

Oceanside Branch
1949 Avenida Del Oro, Suite 106
Oceanside, CA 92056

San Diego Branch
2650 N. Camino del Rio, Suite 209
San Diego, CA 92108

Concord Branch
1070 Concord Ave., Suite 105
Concord, CA 94520

Fremont Branch
3100 Mowry Ave., Suite 403-A
Fremont, CA 94538

CCCS of Kern & Tulare Counties
www.californiacccs.org
(661) 324–9628
(800) 272–2482

Bakersfield Branch
5300 Lennox Ave., Suite 200
Bakersfield, CA 93309

Visalia Branch
718 W. Center St., #C
Visalia, CA 93291

CCCS of San Francisco
www.cccssf.org
(800) 777–7526

San Francisco Branch
595 Market St., 15th Floor
San Francisco, CA 94105

Santa Rosa Branch
70 Stony Point Rd., Suite C
Santa Rosa, CA 95401

CCCS of Santa Clara through Ventura Counties
www.gotdebt.org
(800) 540–2227

Arroyo Grande Branch
1303 E. Grand Ave., Suite 123
Arroyo Grande, CA 93420

Santa Barbara Branch
1221 State St., Suite 4A
Santa Barbara, CA 93101

Camarillo Branch
80 N. Wood Rd., Suite 200
Camarillo, CA 93010

Watsonville Branch
23 E. Beach St., Suite 217
Watsonville, CA 95076

San Jose Branch
1190 S. Bascom Ave., Suite 208
San Jose, CA 95128

CCCS of Orange County
www.cccsoc.org
(800) 213–2227

Anaheim Branch
2450 E. Lincoln
Anaheim, CA 92806

Costa Mesa Branch
2701 Harbor Blvd., Unit E-6
Costa Mesa, CA 92627

Brea Branch
Brea Community Center
695 Madison Way
Brea, CA 92821

Santa Ana Branch
1920 Old Tustin Ave.
Santa Ana, CA 92705

Springboard Nonprofit Consumer Counseling
www.credit.org
(877) 947–3752

Central Valley
Bakersfield Branch
4700 Easton Dr., #1
Bakersfield, CA 93309

Los Angeles
Long Beach Branch
3363 Linden Ave., Suite A
Long Beach, CA 90807

Fresno Branch
443 E. Shields, Suite 18
Fresno, CA 93724

Rosemead Branch
3505 N. Hart Ave.
Rosemead, CA 91770

Orange County
Mission Viejo Branch
28570 Marguerite Pkwy.,
Suite 218
Mission Viejo, CA 92692

Riverside
Hemet Branch
1555 W. Florida Ave.
Hemet, CA 92543

Palm Springs Branch
1001 S. Palm Canyon, #103
Palm Springs, CA 92262

Riverside Branch
4351 Latham St.
Riverside, CA 92501

San Bernardino
San Bernardino Branch
1814 Commercenter West, Suite B
San Bernardino, CA 92408

San Diego
Chula Vista Branch
229 F St., Suite D
Chula Vista, CA 91910

El Cajon Branch
1150 Broadway, Suite 235
El Cajon, CA 92021

San Diego Branch
7710 Balboa Ave., Suite 218-F
San Diego, CA 92111

CCCS of the North Coast
www.cccsnojuggle.org
(800) 762–1811

Arcata Branch
1309 11th St., Suite 104
Arcata, CA 95521

Crescent City Branch
286 M St.
Crescent City, CA 95531

Ukiah Branch
637 S. Orchard
Ukiah, CA 95482

Willits Branch
1155 S. Main St.
Willits, CA 95490

CCCS—Twin City
(530) 674–9729

Yuba City Branch
718 Bridge St., Suite B
Yuba City, CA 95991

CCCS of Southern Oregon
www.cccsso.org
(530) 841–1516

Yreka Branch
1515 S. Oregon St., Suite D
Yreka, CA 96097

Colorado

Money Management International
www.moneymanagement.org
(866) 889–9347

Aurora Branch
10065 E. Harvard Ave., Suite 210
Denver, CO 80231

Highlands Ranch Branch
7120 E. County Line Rd.
Highlands Ranch, CO 80126

Denver (Downtown) Branch
600 S. 17th St., Suite 2800
Denver, CO 80202

Westminster Branch
9101 Harlan St., Suite 150
Westminster, CO 80030

Grand Junction Branch
225 N. 5th St., Suite 703
Grand Junction, CO 81501

CCCS of Northern Colorado & Southeast Wyoming
www.cccsnc.org
(970) 229–0695
(800) 424–2227

Fort Collins Branch
1247 Riverside Ave.
Fort Collins, CO 80524

Loveland Branch
315 E. 7th St.
Loveland, CO 80537

Greeley Branch
918 Thirteenth St., #2
Greeley, CO 80631

Sterling Branch
508 S. 10th Ave.
Sterling, CO 80751

Longmont Branch
2919 17th Ave., #109
Longmont, CO 80501

CCCS of Greater Dallas
www.cccs.net
(800) 249–2227

Colorado Springs (North) Branch
5265 N. Academy Blvd., Suite 1000
Colorado Springs, CO 80918

Pueblo Branch
200 W. 1st St., Suite 302
Pueblo, CO 81003

Colorado Springs (South) Branch
1233 Lake Plaza Dr., Suite A
Colorado Springs, CO 80906

Connecticut

Money Management International
www.moneymanagement.org
(866) 889–9347

East Hartford Branch
225 Pitkin St., Suite 300
East Hartford, CT 06108

Milford Branch
61 Cherry St., Bldg. H,
Suite C-2
Milford, CT 06460

Delaware

CCCS of Maryland & Delaware
www.cccs-inc.org
(800) 642–2227

Dover Branch
375 W. North St.
Dover, DE 19904

Wilmington Branch
2055 Limestone Rd., Suite 212
Wilmington, DE 19808

District of Columbia

Money Management International
www.moneymanagement.org
(866) 889–9347

Washington D.C. Branch
1875 I St. NW, 5th Floor, Suite 537
Washington D.C. 20006

Florida

Family Counseling Center of Brevard
www.fccbrevard.com
(321) 259–1070

Melbourne Branch
507 N. Harbor City Blvd.
Melbourne, FL 32935

Titusville Branch
725 DeLeon Ave.
Titusville, FL 32780

Rockledge Branch
840 Brevard Ave.
Rockledge, FL 32955

Vero Beach Branch
2046 14th Ave.
Vero Beach, FL 32960

CCCS of Greater Atlanta
www.cccsfl.org
(800) 251–2227

Boca Raton Branch
1515 N. Federal Hwy., Suite 200
Boca Raton, FL 33432

Fort Myers Branch
12811 Kenwood Ln., Suite 111
Fort Myers, FL 33907

Brooksville Branch
1 E. Jefferson St.
Brooksville, FL 34601

Leesburg Branch
900 N. 14th St., 2nd Floor
Leesburg, FL 34748

Clearwater Branch
4625 E. Bay Dr., Suite 205
Clearwater, FL 33764

New Port Richey Branch
5945 Florida Ave.
New Port Richey, FL 34652

Dade City Branch
37837 Meridian Ave., Suite 200
Dade City, FL 33525

Orlando Branch
3670 Maguire Blvd., Suite 103
Orlando, FL 32803

Daytona Beach Branch
359 Bill France Blvd.
Daytona Beach, FL 32114

Orlando (South) Branch
6220 S. Orange Blossom Trail,
Suite 115
Orlando, FL 32809

Deltona Branch
2730 Elkcam Blvd.
Deltona, FL 32738

Port Saint Lucie Branch
591 SE Port Saint Lucie Blvd.
Port Saint Lucie, FL 34984

Sarasota Branch
1750 17th St., Bldg. H
Sarasota, FL 34234

Stuart Branch
900 Central Pkwy.
Stuart, FL 34997

Tallahassee Branch
2525 S. Monroe St., Suite 3A
Tallahassee, FL 32301

Tampa Branch
5421 Beaumont Center Blvd.,
Suite 600
Tampa, FL 33634

West Palm Beach Branch
700 S. Dixie Hwy., Suite 103
West Palm Beach, FL 33401

CCCS of Mid-Florida, Inc.
www.cccsmidflorida.com
(800) 245–1865

Gainesville Branch
1227 NW 16th Ave.
Gainesville, FL 32601

Inverness Branch
508 W. Main St.
Inverness, FL 34450

Lake City Branch
725 SE Baya Dr., Suite 107
Lake City, FL 32025

Ocala Branch
1539 NE 22nd Ave.
Ocala, FL 34470

Palatka Branch
Bank of America
620 US Hwy. 19 South
Palatka, FL 32177

CCCS of West Florida, Inc.
www.cccswfl.org
(888) 475–8697

Crestview Branch
212 N. Wilson St.
Crestview, FL 32536

De Funiak Springs Branch
171 N. 9th St.
De Funiak Springs, FL 32433

Fort Walton Beach Branch
913 N. Beal Pkwy., Unit H
Fort Walton Beach, FL 32547

Hialeah Branch
1800 W. 49th St., #303
Hialeah, FL 33012

Panama City Branch
625 Hwy. 231
Panama City, FL 32401

Pensacola Branch
14 Palafox Pl.
Pensacola, FL 32502

Family Foundations
www.familyfoundations.org
(904) 396–4846
(888) 444–0046

Jacksonville Branch
1639 Atlantic Blvd.
Jacksonville, FL 32207

Orange Park Branch
1409 Kingsley Ave.
Orange Park, FL 32073

Jacksonville Beach Branch
1316 N. Third St.
Jacksonville Beach, FL 32250

St. Augustine Branch
Bank of America
60 Cathedral Pl.
St. Augustine, FL 32084

Consumer Debt Counselors, Inc.
www.consumerdebtcounselors.com
(800) 820–9232

Port Charlotte Branch
4055 Tamiami Trail, Suite 23
Port Charlotte, FL 33953

Winter Park Branch
222 S. Pennsylvania Ave.,
Suite 100
Winter Park, FL 32789

CCCS of South Florida
www.credit-counseling.org
(800) 355–2227

Homestead Branch
301 Civic Ct.
Homestead, FL 33030

Plantation Branch
1333 S. University Dr., Suite 210
Fort Lauderdale, FL 33324

Lighthouse Point Branch
3170 N. Federal Hwy., Suite 103E
Lighthouse Point, FL 33064

South Dade Branch
12651 S. Dixie Hwy., Suite 303
Miami, FL 33156

Miami Branch
1175 NE 125th St., Suite 413
Miami, FL 33161

Georgia

CCCS of Greater Atlanta
www.cccsinc.org
(800) 251–2227

Atlanta Branch
100 Edgewood Ave. SE,
Suite 1800
Atlanta, GA 30303

Marietta Branch
1640 Powers Ferry Rd., Bldg. 14, Suite 100
Marietta, GA 30067

Decatur Branch
1 W. Court Sq., Suite 140
Decatur, GA 30030

Rome Branch
413 Shorter Ave. SW, Suite 101
Rome, GA 30165

Douglasville Branch
4935 Stewart Mill Rd., Suite 103
Douglasville, GA 30135

Stockbridge Branch
245 Village Center Pkwy.
Stockbridge, GA 30281

Gainesville Branch
322 Oak St., Suite 3
Gainesville, GA 30501

CCCS of Middle Georgia, Inc.
www.cccsmacon.org
(800) 446–7123

Macon Branch
901 Washington Ave.
Macon, GA 31201

Warner Robins Branch
748 N. Houston Rd., Suite H
Warner Robins, GA 31093

CCCS of the Savannah Area, Inc.
www.cccssavannah.org
(912) 691–2227
(800) 821–4040

Brunswick Branch
501 Gloucester St., Suite 202
Brunswick, GA 31520

Savannah Branch
7505 Waters Ave., Suite C-11
Savannah, GA 31406

Hinesville Branch
220 Fraser Dr.
Hinesville, GA 31313

Statesboro Branch
515 Denmark St.
Statesboro, GA 31406

CCCS of Southwest Georgia
www.cccsalbany.org
(229) 883–0909
(800) 309–3358

Albany Branch
409 N. Jackson St.
Albany, GA 31701

Valdosta Branch
509 N. Patterson St., Suite 304
Valdosta, GA 31062

The Family Center
www.realpages.com/sites/familycenter
(706) 327–3239

Columbus Branch
1350 15th Ave.
Columbus, GA 31902

LaGrange Branch
309 Mooty Bridge Rd., Suite C
LaGrange, GA 30240

CCCS of the Central Savannah River Area
www.cccsaugusta.org
(800) 736–0033

Augusta Branch
1341 Druid Park Ave.
Augusta, GA 30904

Hawaii

CCCS of Hawaii
www.cccsofhawaii.org
(808) 532–3225
(800) 801–5999

Big Island Branch
632 Kinoole St.
Hilo, HI 96720

Oahu Branch
1164 Bishop St., Suite 1614
Honolulu, HI 96813

Maui Branch
95 Mahalani St., Suite 6
Wailuku, HI 96793

Idaho

Money Management International
www.moneymanagement.org
(866) 889–9347

Coeur d'Alene Branch
1801 Lincoln Way, Suite 6
Coeur d'Alene, ID 83814

CCCS of Northern Idaho
www.cccsnid.org
(208) 746–0127
(800) 556–0127

Lewiston Branch
1113 Main St.
Lewiston, ID 83501

Illinois

Family Counseling Service of Aurora
www.aurorafcs.org
(630) 844–3327
(800) 349–1451

Aurora Branch
70 S. River St., Suite 2
Aurora, IL 60506

Money Management International
www.moneymanagement.org
(866) 889–9347

Chicago Branch
70 East Lake St., Suite 1115
Chicago, IL 60601

Oak Park Branch
1515 N. Harlem Ave., Suite 205
Oak Park, IL 60302

Glen Ellyn Branch
1200 Roosevelt Rd., Suite 108
Glen Ellyn, IL 60137

Peoria Branch
The Commerce Bldg.
416 Main St., Suite 920
Peoria, IL, 60602

Rockford Branch
129 S. Phelps Ave., Suite 811
Rockford, IL 61108

Tinley Park Branch
16860 S. Oak Park Ave., Suite 203
Tinley Park, IL 60477

Rolling Meadows Branch
3601 Algonquin Rd., Suite 230
Rolling Meadows, IL 60008

Chestnut Credit Counseling Services
www.chestnut.org
(800) 615–3022

Belleville Branch
12 N. 64th St.
Belleville, IL 62223

Joliet Branch
151 Springfield Ave., Suite C
Joliet, IL 60435

Bloomington Branch
1003 Martin Luther King Dr.
Bloomington, IL 61701

Maryville Branch
2148 Vadalabene Dr.
Maryville, IL 62062

Granite City Branch
50 Northgate Industrial Dr.
Granite City, IL 62040

Family Service Association of Greater Elgin Area
www.fsaelgin.org/cccs.htm
(847) 695–3680

Elgin Branch
22 Spring St.
Elgin, IL 60120

Streamwood Branch
1535 Burgundy Pkwy.
Streamwood, IL 60107

Hoffman Estates Branch
1900 Hassell Rd.
Hoffman Estates, IL 60195

CCCS of McHenry County, Inc.
www.illinoiscccs.org
(815) 338–5757

Woodstock Branch
400 Russel Ct.
Woodstock, IL 60098

GreenPath Debt Solutions
www.greenpath.com
(800) 550–1961

Moline Branch
5306 Avenue of the Cities, Suite A
Moline, IL 61265

ClearPoint Financial Solutions, Inc.
www.clearpointcreditcounselingsolutions.org
(877) 422–9040

Marion Branch
1616 W. Main St., Suite 200
Marion, IL 62959

Mt. Vernon Branch
123 S. 10th St., Suite 205
Mt. Vernon, IL 62864

Quincy Branch
1511 S. 12th St.
Quincy, IL 62301

Springfield Branch
975 S. Durkin Dr.
Springfield, IL 62704

Swansea Branch
4972 Benchmark Center,
Suite 300
Swansea, IL 62226

Indiana

Momentive CCCS
www.momentive.org
(888) 711–7227

Anderson Branch
931 Meridian Plaza, Suite 501
Anderson, IN 46016

Bloomington Branch
205 N. College, Suite 014
Bloomington, IN 47404

Columbus Branch
United Way Center
1531 13th St., Suite 1360
Columbus, IN 47201

Evansville Branch
715 First Ave., 3rd Floor
Evansville, IN 47710

Indianapolis Branch
615 N. Alabama St., Suite 134
Indianapolis, IN 46204

Muncie Branch
2803 N. Oakwood
Muncie, IN 47304

Terre Haute Branch
2001 N. 19th St.
Terre Haute, IN 47804

CCCS of Northeastern Indiana
www.financialhope.org
(260) 432–8200
(800) 432–0420

Auburn Branch
117 W. 9th St.
Auburn, IN 46706

Warsaw Branch
850 N. Harrison St.
Warsaw, IN 46580

Fort Wayne Branch
4105 W. Jefferson Blvd.
Fort Wayne, IN 46804

CCCS of Northwest Indiana
www.cccsnwi.org
(219) 980–4800
(800) 982–4801

Gary Branch
3637 Grant St.
Gary, IN 46408

GreenPath Debt Solutions
www.greenpath.com
(800) 550–1961

Elkhart Branch
500 N. Nappanee St., Suite 7A
Elkhart, IN 46514

Mishawaka Branch
245 Edison Rd., Suite 230
Mishawaka, IN 46545

Graceworks Lutheran Services
www.graceworks.org/cccs
(800) 377–2432

Richmond Branch
First English Lutheran Church
2727 E. Main St.
Richmond, IN 47374

Family Services, Inc.
www.fsilafayette.org
(765) 423–5361
(800) 875–5361

Lafayette Branch
615 N. 18th St., Suite 201
Lafayette, IN 47904

CCCS of New Albany
www.credit-counseling.org
(800) 355–2227

New Albany Branch
3602 Northgate Ct., Suite 37A
New Albany, IN 47150

Iowa

CCCS of Nebraska, Inc.
www.cccsn.org

Des Moines Branch
6200 Aurora Ave., Suite 504
Urbandale, IA 50322

CCCS of Northeastern Iowa
www.cccsia.org
(800) 714–4388

Ames Branch
1608 S. Duff Ave., Suite 300
Ames, IA 50010

Grinnell Branch
1030 Broad St.
Grinnell, IA 50112

Dubuque Branch
810 Locust St.
Dubuque, IA 52001

Marshalltown Branch
30 W. Main St.
Marshalltown, IA 50158

Forest City Branch
102 N. 4th St.
Forest City, IA 50436

Mason City Branch
404 S. Monroe Ave.
Mason City, IA 50401

Waterloo Branch
1003 W. Fourth St.
Waterloo, IA 50702

Horizons CCCS
www.horizonscccs.org
(800) 826–3574

Cedar Rapids Branch
819 5th St. SE
Cedar Rapids, IA 52406

Coralville Branch
2000 James St.
Coralville, IA 52441

Kansas

CCCS of Greater Kansas City & Mid-Missouri
www.credit-counseling.org
(800) 355–2227

Olathe Branch
15795 S. Mahaffie St.,
Suite 102
Olathe, KS 66062

Overland Park Branch
8826 Santa Fe Dr., Suite 110
Overland Park, KS 66212

CCCS of Springfield/Joplin/West Plains
www.cccsoftheozarks.org
(800) 882–0808

Pittsburg Branch
US Bank Bldg.
306 N. Broadway St.
Pittsburg, KS 66762

CCC, Inc.
www.kscccs.org
(800) 279–2227

Garden City Branch
1521 E. Fulton St.
Garden City, KS 67846

Hutchinson Branch
1 E. 9th Ave., Suite 201
Hutchinson, KS 67501

Hays Branch
1200 N. Main St.
Hays, KS 67601

Salina Branch
1201 W. Walnut St.
Salina, KS 67401

Wichita Branch
300 W. Douglas Ave., Suite 900
Wichita, KS 67202

Housing and Credit Counseling, Inc.
www.hcci-ks.org
(785) 234–0217
(800) 383–0217

Emporia Branch
625 Merchant St., Suite 205
Emporia, KS 66801

Manhattan Branch
2601 Anderson Ave., #203
Manhattan, KS 66502

Lawrence Branch
2518 SW Ridge Ct.
Lawrence, KS 66046

Topeka Branch
1195 SW Buchanan St.,
Suite 101
Topeka, KS 66604

Kentucky

CCCS of Louisville
www.credit-counseling.org
(800) 355–2227

Bowling Green Branch
1725 Ashley Circle, Suite 107
Bowling Green, KY 42104

Louisville Branch
2100 Gardiner Ln., Suite 103A
Louisville, KY 40205

Elizabethtown Branch
950 N. Mulberry St., Suite 220
Elizabethtown, KY 42701

Louisville (East) Branch
11492 Bluegrass Pkwy., Suite 110
Louisville, KY 40299

CCCS of Greater Cincinnati, Inc.
www.credit-counseling.org
(800) 355–2227

Florence Branch
United Way Bldg.
11 Shelby St.
Florence, KY 41042

CCCS of Central Kentucky
www.credit-counseling.org
(800) 355–2227

Frankfort Branch
417 High St., Suite A
Frankfort, KY 40601

Pikeville Branch
131 Main St., 2nd Floor
Pikeville, KY 41501

Lexington Branch
2265 Harrodsburg Rd.,
Suite 303
Lexington, KY 40504

Richmond Branch
200 E. Main St., 2nd Floor
Richmond, KY 40475

Momentive CCCS
www.momentive.org
(888) 711–7227

Owensboro Branch
920 Frederica St., Suite 213
Owensboro, KY 42301

ClearPoint Financial Solutions, Inc.
www.clearpointcreditcounselingsolutions.org
(877) 422–9040

Paducah Branch
100 Fountain Dr., Suite 200
Paducah, KY 42001

Louisiana

Money Management International
www.moneymanagement.org
(866) 889–9347

Alexandria Branch
1106 MacArthur Dr., Suite 2
Alexandria, LA 71303

Bossier City Branch
700 Northgate Rd.
Bossier City, LA 71112

Baton Rouge Branch
615 Chevelle Ct.
Baton Rouge, LA 70806

Lafayette Branch
117 Liberty Ave.
Lafayette, LA 70508

Lake Charles Branch
2021 Oak Park Blvd.
Lake Charles, LA 70601

Monroe Branch
2912 Evangeline St.
Monroe, LA 71201

Shreveport Branch
8575 Business Park Dr.
Shreveport, LA 71105

Greater New Orleans
Houma Branch
1340 W. Tunnel Blvd., Suite 500
Houma, LA 70360

Metairie Branch
4051 Veterans Memorial Blvd.,
Suite 226
Metairie, LA 70002

New Orleans Branch
1215 Prytania St., Suite 424
New Orleans, LA 70130

Slidell Branch
1338 Gause Blvd., Suite 202
Slidell, LA 70458

Consumer Debt Counselors, Inc.
www.consumerdebtcounselors.com
(800) 820–9232

Baton Rouge Branch
13000 Justice Ave., Suite 11
Baton Rouge, LA 70816

Lafayette Branch
106 Oil Center Dr., Suite 102M
Lafayette, LA 70503

Metairie Branch
3925 N. I-10 Service Rd. West,
Suite 222
Metairie, LA 70002

Maine

Money Management International
www.moneymanagement.org
(866) 889–9347

Auburn Branch
250 Center St., Suite 205
Auburn, ME 04210

Augusta Branch
1 Bangor St.
Augusta, ME 04330

Bangor Branch
175 Exchange St.
Bangor, ME 04401

South Portland Branch
111 Wescott Rd.
South Portland, ME 04106

Biddeford Park Branch
407 Alfred Rd., Park 111,
Suite 202
Biddeford, ME 04005

Maryland

CCCS of Maryland & Delaware
www.cccs-inc.org
(800) 642–2227

Baltimore Branch
757 Frederick Rd.
Baltimore, MD 21228

Essex Branch
408 Eastern Blvd.
Essex, MD 21221

Bel Air Branch
1201 Agora Dr., Suite 2D
Bel Air, Maryland 21014

Owings Mills Branch
10220 S. Dolfield Rd., Suite 105
Owings Mills, MD 21117

Brooklyn Park Branch
5410 Ritchie Hwy., Suite B
Baltimore, MD 21225

Parkville Branch
7905-B Harford Rd.
Parkville, MD 21234

Easton Branch
219 Marlboro Rd., Suite 46
Easton, MD 21601

Salisbury Branch
242 Tilghman Rd., Suite 242
Salisbury, MD 21804

ClearPoint Financial Solutions, Inc.
www.clearpointcreditcounselingsolutions.org
(877) 422–9040

Lanham Branch
9344 Lanham Severn Rd., Suite 205
Lanham, MD 20706

Money Management International
www.moneymanagement.org
(866) 889–9347

Frederick Branch
1003 W. 7th St., Suite 404
Frederick, MD 21701

Rockville Branch
15847 Crabbs Branch Way
Rockville, MD 20855

Massachusetts

Money Management International
www.moneymanagement.org
(866) 889–9347

Amherst Branch
409 Main St., Suite 105
Amherst, MA 01002

Beverly Branch
100 Cummings Center,
Suite S-311H
Beverly, MA 01915

Boston Branch
8 Winter St., 7th Floor
Boston, MA 02108

Lowell Branch
40 Central St.
Lowell, MA 01852

New Bedford Branch
888 Purchase St.
New Bedford, MA 02740

Pittsfield Branch
34 Depot St.
Pittsfield, MA 01202

Randolph Branch
247 Main St., Suite 200
Randolph, MA 02368

Springfield Branch
59 Interstate Dr., Suite G
West Springfield, MA 01089

Woburn Branch
800 W. Cummings Park,
Suite 1075
Woburn, MA 01801

Worcester Branch
340 Main St., Suite 813
Worcester, MA 01608

Michigan

GreenPath Debt Solutions
www.greenpath.com
(800) 550–1961

Ann Arbor Branch
315 E. Eisenhower, Suite 206
Ann Arbor, MI 48108

Battle Creek Branch
131 E. Columbia Ave., Suite 112
Battle Creek, MI 49015

Brighton Branch
211 N. First St., Suite 300
Brighton, MI 48116

Detroit Branch
2111 Woodward Ave., Suite 906
Detroit, MI 48201

Farmington Hills Branch
38505 Country Club Dr., Suite 120
Farmington Hills, MI 48331

Flint Branch
2222 S. Linden Rd., Suite D
Flint, MI 48532

Gaylord Branch
810 S. Otsego Ave., Suite 105
Gaylord, MI 49735

Grand Rapids Branch
3210 Eagle Run Dr. NE,
Suite 102
Grand Rapids, MI 49525

Ironwood Branch
629 W. Cloverland Dr., Suite 9
Ironwood, MI 49938

Jackson Branch
211 W. Ganson
Jackson, MI 49201

Lansing Branch
612 S. Creyts Rd., Suite C
Lansing, MI 48917

Marquette Branch
712 Chippewa Sq.,
Suite 102
Marquette, MI 49855

Monroe Branch
25 S. Monroe St., Suite 312
Monroe, MI 48161

Muskegon Branch
800 Ellis Rd., Suite 269
Muskegon, MI 49441

Port Huron Branch
3051 Commerce Dr., Suite 3
Fort Gratiot, MI 48059

Portage Branch
7127 S. Westnedge Ave., Suite 5C
Portage, MI 49081

Roseville Branch
27085 Gratiot Ave., Suite 103
Roseville, MI 48066

Saginaw Branch
4600 Fashion Sq. Blvd.,
Suite 202
Saginaw, MI 48604

Southfield Branch
26555 Evergreen Rd.,
Suite 1060
Southfield, MI 48076

Taylor Branch
8750 S. Telegraph Rd.,
Suite 100
Taylor, MI 48180

Traverse City Branch
10850 E. Traverse Hwy., Suite 2280
Traverse City, MI 49684

Troy Branch
Northfield Plaza II
5700 Crooks Rd., Suite 202
Troy, MI 48098

Utica Branch
11111 Hall Rd., Suite 422
Utica, MI 48317

Westland Branch
38545 Ford Rd., Suite 202
Westland, MI 48185

Minnesota

The Village Family Service Center
www.thevillagefamily.org
(800) 627–8220

Alexandria Branch
460 Northside Dr., Suite 5
Alexandria, MN 56308

Brainerd Branch
200 S. 6th St.
Brainerd, MN 56401

Crystal Branch
7000 N. 57th Ave., Suite 105
Crystal, MN 55428

Detroit Lakes Branch
910 Lincoln Ave.
Detroit Lakes, MN 56501

Fergus Falls Branch
220 W. Washington Ave., Suite 104
Fergus Falls, MN 56537

Moorhead Branch
1401 S. 8th St.
Moorhead, MN 56560

St. Cloud Branch
3950 N. 3rd St.
St. Cloud, MN 56303

Lutheran Social Services of Minnesota
www.lssmn.org
(888) 577–2227

Brainerd Branch
716 E St.
Brainerd, MN 56401

Minneapolis Branch
2414 Park Ave.
Minneapolis, MN 55404

Duluth Branch
424 W. Superior St.,
Suite 600
Duluth, MN 55802

St. Paul Branch
590 Park St., Suite 310
St. Paul, MN 55103

Eveleth Branch
Wells Fargo Bank Bldg.
302 Grant Ave.
Eveleth, MN 55734

St. Paul Branch
965 Payne Ave.
St. Paul, MN 55130

Hopkins Branch
33 S. Tenth Ave., Suite 150
Hopkins, MN 55343

Willmar Branch
1601 Hwy. 12 East, Suite 6
Willmar, MN 56201

Mankato Branch
710 S. Second St.
Mankato, MN 56001

FamilyMeans CCCS
www.familymeans.org
(800) 780–2890

Minneapolis Branch
3433 NE Broadway St., Suite 245
Minneapolis, MN 55413

Stillwater Branch
1875 Northwestern Ave.
Stillwater, MN 55082

Minnetonka Branch
10560 Wayzata Blvd., Suite 11
Minnetonka, MN 55305

Rochester Branch
903 W. Center St., Suite 200
Rochester, MN 55902

Mississippi

Money Management International
www.moneymanagement.org
(866) 346–2227

Biloxi Branch
2318 Pass Rd., Suite 2
Biloxi, MS 39531

Tupelo Branch
1018 N. Gloster St., Suite H
Tupelo, MS 38804

CCCS of Greater Atlanta
www.cccsatl.org
(800) 251–2227

Jackson Branch
2906 N. State St., Suite 204
Jackson, MS 39216

Family Service Agency—CCCS
www.helpingfamilies.org
(800) 255–2227

Southaven Branch
7075 Golden Oaks Loop West,
Suite 12
Southaven, MS 38671

Missouri

ClearPoint Financial Solutions, Inc.
www.clearpointcreditcounselingsolutions.org
(877) 422–9040

Arnold Branch
19 Fox Valley Center
Arnold, MO 63010

Columbia Branch
2401 Bernadette Dr., Suite 115
Columbia, MO 65203

Cape Girardeau Branch
1301 N. Kingshighway St.
Cape Girardeau, MO 63701

Florissant Branch
493 Rue St. Francois, Suite 6
Florissant, MO 63031

Poplar Bluff Branch
948 Lester St., Suite 5
Poplar Bluff, MO 63901

St. Louis Branch
1300 Hampton Ave.
St. Louis, MO 63139

St. Charles Branch
1600 Heritage Landing, Suite 104
St. Charles, MO 63303

CCCS of Springfield/Joplin/West Plains
www.cccsoftheozarks.org
(800) 882–0808

Branson Branch
520 W. Main St.
Branson, MO 65616

Springfield (Glenstone) Branch
1515 S. Glenstone Ave.
Springfield, MO 65804

Joplin Branch
3130 Wisconsin Ave., Suite 4
Joplin, MO 64804

Springfield (Campbell) Branch
1055 S. Campbell Ave.
Springfield, MO 65807

Lebanon Branch
US Bank Bldg.
201 N. Jefferson Ave.
Lebanon, MO 65536

Thayer Branch
Bank of Thayer
116 E. Chestnut St.
Thayer, MO 65791

Monett Branch
US Bank Bldg.
522 E. Broadway St.
Monett, MO 65708

West Plains Branch
1524 Porter Wagoner Blvd.
West Plains, MO 65775

CCCS of Greater Kansas City & Mid-Missouri
www.credit-counseling.org
(800) 355–2227

Columbia Branch
1900 N. Providence, Suite 309
Columbia, MO 65202

Kansas City Branch
9300 Troost Ave.
Kansas City, MO 64131

Independence Branch
3737 S. Elizabeth St., Suite 103
Independence, MO 64057

St. Joseph Branch
724 N. Belt Hwy.
St. Joseph, MO 64506

Montana

Rural Dynamics Inc.
www.cccsmt.org
(877) 275–2227

Bozeman Branch
8645 Huffine Ln., Suite 3
Bozeman, MT 59718

Helena Branch
910 East Lyndale Ave., Suite A
Helena, MT 59601

Butte Branch
800 E. Front St.
Butte, MT 59701

Kalispell Branch
690 N. Meridian, Suite 206
Kalispell, MT 59901

Great Falls Branch
2022 Central Ave.
Great Falls, MT 59403

Missoula Branch
1515 Fairview Ave., Suite 220
Missoula, MT 59801

Nebraska

CCCS of Nebraska, Inc.
www.cccsn.org
(877) 494–2227

Grand Island Branch
2121 N. Webb Rd., Suite 307
Grand Island, NE 68802

North Platte Branch
509 E. 4th St., Suite F
North Platte, NE 69103

Lincoln Branch
1001 S. 70th St., Suite 200
Lincoln, NE 68505

Omaha (Indian Hills) Branch
8805 Indian Hills Dr., Suite 105
Omaha, NE 68114

Norfolk Branch
700 ½ W. Benjamin Ave.
Norfolk, NE 68701

Omaha Branch
11225 Davenport St., Suite 108
Omaha, NE 68154

Nevada

CCCS of Southern Nevada & Utah
www.cccsnevada.org
(800) 451–4505

Henderson Branch
2920 N. Green Valley Pkwy.
Henderson, NV 89014

Laughlin Branch
55 Civic Way, No. 2
Laughlin, NV 89029

Las Vegas Branch
2650 S. Jones Blvd.
Las Vegas, NV 89146

Reno Branch
3100 Mill St., Suite 111
Reno, NV 89502

CCCS of Northern Nevada
www.fcsnv.org
(800) 275–0137

Reno Branch
575 E. Plumb Ln., Suite 101
Reno, NV 89502

New Hampshire

CCCS of New Hampshire & Vermont
www.cccsnh-vt.org
(800) 327–6778

Concord Branch
105 Loudon Rd., Bldg. #1
Concord, NH 03302

Keene Branch
64 Main St.
Keene, NH 03431

Dover Branch
92 Washington St.,
Suite 213
Dover, NH 03820

Laconia Branch
585 Union Ave.
Laconia, NH 03246

Exeter Branch
127 Water St.
Exeter, NH 03833

Lebanon Branch
1 Court St., 3rd Floor
Lebanon, NH 03766

Littleton Branch
113 Cottage St.
Littleton, NH 03561

Nashua Branch
28 Concord St.
Nashua, NH 03060

Manchester Branch
114 Bay St.
Manchester, NH 03104

Tilton Branch
608 W. Main St.
Tilton, NH 03276

Money Management International
www.moneymanagement.org
(866) 346–2227

Portsmouth Branch
Northeast Credit Union
100 Borthwick Ave.
Portsmouth, NH 03802

New Jersey

CCCS of New Jersey
www.cccsnj.org
(888) 726–3260

Cedar Knolls Branch
185 Ridgedale Ave.
Cedar Knolls, NJ 07927

Somerville Branch
145 W. Main St.
Somerville, NJ 08876

Ridgewood Branch
148 Prospect St.
Ridgewood, NJ 07450

CCCS of Delaware Valley
www.cccsdv.org
(800) 989–2227

Cherry Hill Branch
1 Cherry Hill, Suite 215
Cherry Hill, NJ 08002

Money Management International
www.moneymanagement.org
(866) 346–2227

South Jersey Branch
3073 English Creek Ave., Suite 3
Egg Harbor Township, NJ 08234

Turnersville Branch
860 Rt. 168, Suite 104
Turnersville, NJ 08012

Tinton Falls Branch
106 Apple St., Suite 105
Tinton Falls, NJ 07724

CCCS of Central New Jersey
www.cccscentralnj.com
(888) 379–0604

Hamilton Branch
1931 Nottingham Way
Hamilton, NJ 08619

New Mexico

CCCS of the YWCA—Paso Del Norte Region
www.ywcaelpaso.org
(888) 533–7502

Alamogordo Branch
700 E. First St., Suite 713
Alamogordo, NM 88310

Las Cruces Branch
1401 S. Don Roser Dr.,
Bldg. A, Suite 1
Las Cruces, NM 88011

Money Management International
www.moneymanagement.org
(866) 346–2227

Albuquerque (Central) Branch
2727 San Pedro NE, Suite 117
Albuquerque, NM 87110

Farmington Branch
3001 Northridge Dr., Suite A
Farmington, NM 87401

Albuquerque (Promenade) Branch
5200 Eubank Blvd. NE
Albuquerque, NM 87111

Las Cruces Branch
1065 S. Main St., Suite B-12
Las Cruces, NM 88005

Santa Fe Branch
228 St. Francis Dr., Suite C-2
Santa Fe, NM 87501

CCCS of Greater Dallas
www.cccs.net
(800) 538–2227

Clovis Branch
1800 Sheffield Dr., Suite B
Clovis, NM 88101

New York

CCCS of Central New York
www.credithelpny.org
(800) 479–6026

Albany Branch
2 Computer Dr. West
Albany, NY 12205

Utica Branch
289 Genesee St.
Utica, NY 13501

Binghamton Branch
49 Court St.
Binghamton, NY 13901

Watertown Branch
215 Washington St.,
Suite B-5
Watertown, NY 13601

Syracuse Branch
5794 Widewaters Pkwy.
Syracuse, NY 13214

GreenPath Debt Solutions
www.greenpath.com
(800) 550–1961

Bronx Branch
3250 Westchester Ave., Suite 111
Bronx, NY 10461

Hauppauge Branch
700 Veterans Memorial Hwy., Suite 40
Hauppauge, NY 11788

Brooklyn Branch
175 Remsen St., Suite 1102
Brooklyn, NY 11201

Jericho Branch
380 N. Broadway, Suite 304
Jericho, NY 11753

Manhattan Branch
120 Broadway, Suite 935
New York, NY 10271

Manhattan (34th St.) Branch
One Penn Plaza
250 W. 34th St., Suite 2108
New York, NY 10119

Queens Branch
80–02 Kew Gardens Rd.,
Suite 710
Queens, NY 11415

Money Management International
www.moneymanagement.org
(866) 346–2227

Bronx Branch
888 Grand Concourse, Suite 1K
Bronx, NY 10451

Brooklyn Branch
26 Court St., Suite 1801
Brooklyn, NY 11201

Manhattan Branch
11 Penn Plaza, Suite 5148
New York, NY 10001

Queens Branch
88–32 Sutphin Blvd.
Queens, NY 11435

CCCS of Buffalo, Inc.
www.cccsbuff.org
(716) 712–2060
(800) 926–9685

Buffalo Branch
43 Court St.
Buffalo, NY 14202

West Seneca Branch
40 W. Gardenville Pkwy.,
Suite 300
Buffalo, NY 14224

North Carolina

CCCS of Greater Greensboro
www.thedebtdoc.com
(888) 755–2227

Asheboro Branch
135 Sunset Ave.
Asheboro, NC 27205

Burlington Branch
719 Hermitage Rd.
Burlington, NC 27215

Greensboro Branch
315 E. Washington St.
Greensboro, NC 27401

Wentworth Branch
525 NC 65
Wentworth, NC 27320

High Point Branch
1401 Long St.
High Point, NC 27262

Yanceyville Branch
331 Piedmont Dr.
Yanceyville, NC 27379

OnTrack Financial Education & Counseling
www.cccsofwnc.org
(800) 737–5485

Asheville Branch
50 S. French Broad Ave.,
Suite 227
Asheville, NC 28801

Marion Branch
McDowell Public Library
100 W. Court St.
Marion, NC 28752

Boone Branch
207 Winklers Creek Rd.
Boone, NC 28607

Sylva Branch
5 S. Maple St.
Sylva, NC 28779

Franklin Branch
Macon Savings Bank
50 W. Main St.
Franklin, NC 28734

Waynesville Branch
First Citizens Bank
196 Walnut St.
Waynesville, NC 28786

Hendersonville Branch
722 W. 5th Ave.
Hendersonville, NC 28739

ClearPoint Financial Solutions, Inc.
www.clearpointcreditcounselingsolutions.org
(877) 422–9040

Charlotte Branch
6047 Tyvola Glen Circle, Suite 243
Charlotte, NC 28217

Greenville Branch
315 Clifton St., Suite G
Greenville, NC 27858

Greensboro Branch
338 N. Elm St., Suite 303
Greensboro, NC 27401

Raleigh Branch
4030 Wake Forest Rd., Suite 300
Raleigh, NC 27609

United Family Services
www.unitedfamilyservices.org
(704) 332–9034

Charlotte Branch
601 E. Fifth St., Suite 400
Charlotte, NC 28202

Lake Norman Branch
9624 Bailey Rd., Suite 290
Cornelius, NC 28031

Concord Branch
952 Copperfield Blvd.
Concord, NC 28025

Monroe Branch
604 Lancaster Ave.
Monroe, NC 28112

Family Service, Inc.
(888) 213–8853

Gastonia Branch
214 E. Franklin Blvd.
Gastonia, NC 28052

CCCS of Catawba Valley
www.fgcservices.com
(828) 322–7161

Hickory Branch
17 US Highway 70 SE
Hickory, NC 28602

Morganton Branch
720 E. Union St.
Morganton, NC 28655

Family Services of Davidson County
www.fsdc.org
(336) 249–0237

Lexington Branch
1303 Greensboro St. Ext.
Lexington, NC 27295

CCCS of the Carolina Foothills
www.cccsofcf.org
(828) 286–7062

Spindale Branch
200 Ohio St.
Spindale, NC 28160

Cumberland Community Action Program
www.ccap-inc.org
(888) 381–3720

Coastal Carolina Branch
233 Middle St., Suite 206
New Bern, NC 28563

Sanford Branch
403 W. Makepeace St.
Sanford, NC 27330

Fayetteville Branch
316 Green St.
Fayetteville, NC 28302

Smithfield Branch
245 College Rd.
Smithfield, NC 27577

Kinston Branch
327 N. Queen St., Suite 107
Kinston, NC 28501

Southern Pines Branch
235 E. Pennsylvania Ave.
Southern Pines, NC 28387

Lumberton Branch
4850 Fayetteville Rd., Suite 18
Lumberton, NC 28358

Wilmington Branch
206 N. Fourth St., Unit 7
Wilmington, NC 28401

Triangle Family Services
www.tfsnc.org
(919) 821–0790 x307

Raleigh Branch
401 Hillsborough St.
Raleigh, NC 27603

CCCS of Forsyth County, Inc.
www.cccsforsyth.org
(888) 474–8015

Iredell County Branch
1835 Davie Ave., Suite 401
Statesville, NC 28677

Winston-Salem Branch
8064 North Point Blvd.,
Suite 204
Winston-Salem, NC 27106

Kernersville Branch
431 Bodenhamer St.
Kernersville, NC 27284

Yadkinville Branch
246 E. Main St.
Yadkinville, NC 27055

Mocksville Branch
773 Sanford Ave.
Mocksville, NC 27028

North Dakota

The Village Family Service Center
www.thevillagefamily.org
(800) 627–8220

Bismarck Branch
411 N. 4th St., Suite 10
Bismarck, ND 58501

Jamestown Branch
300 2nd Ave. NE, Suite 217
Jamestown, ND 58401

Fargo Branch
1201 S. 25th St.
Fargo, ND 58103

Minot Branch
Bremer Bank Bldg.
20 1st St. SW, Suite 250
Minot, ND 58701

Grand Forks Branch
1726 S. Washington St.,
Suite 33A
Grand Forks, ND 58201

Ohio

CCCS of the Midwest
www.credit-counseling.org
(800) 355–2227

Akron Branch
2569 Romig Rd.
Akron, OH 44320

Beachwood Branch
21403 Chagrin Blvd., Suite 102
Beachwood, OH 44122

Alliance Branch
1085 W. State St.
Alliance, OH 44601

Blue Ash Branch
9545 Kenwood Rd., Suite 204
Cincinnati, Ohio 45242

Ashtabula Branch
4200 Park Ave., 3rd Floor
Ashtabula, OH 44004

Boardman Branch
8261 Market St., Suite K
Boardman, OH 44512

Batavia Branch
1147 Cincinnati-Batavia Pike
Batavia, OH 45103

Canton Branch
2800 N. Market Ave., Suite 18
Canton, OH 44714

Cincinnati Branch
9600 Colerain Ave., Suite 405
Cincinnati, OH 45251

Cleveland Branch
2800 Euclid Ave., Suite 101
Cleveland, OH 44115

Columbus Branch
4500 E. Broad St.
Columbus, OH 43213

Grove City Branch
3894 Broadway
Grove City, OH 43123

Hilliard Branch
5555 Renner Rd.
Columbus, OH 43228

Mansfield Branch
1 Marion Ave., Suite 307
Mansfield, OH 44903

Marysville Branch
246 W. 5th St., Suite 103
Marysville, OH 43040

Mason Branch
7577 Central Park Blvd., Suite 226C
Mason, OH 45040

Medina Branch
445 W. Liberty St., Suite 230
Medina, OH 44256

Newark Branch
23 S. Park Pl., Suite 210
Newark, OH 43058

Parma Branch
5339 Ridge Rd., Suite 201
Parma, OH 44129

Steubenville Branch
346 S. Hollywood Blvd.
Steubenville, OH 43952

Streetsboro Branch
9205 State Rt. 43, Suite 104
Streetsboro, OH 44241

Toledo Branch
457 S. Reynolds Rd.
Toledo, OH 43615

Warren Branch
554 N. Park Ave.
Warren, OH 44481

Zanesville Branch
503 Main St.
Zanesville, OH 43701

Family & Community Services
www.portagefamilies.org
(800) 258–0694

Akron Branch
212 Exchange St.
Akron, OH 44304

East Liverpool Branch
Kent State University
400 E. 4th St.
East Liverpool, OH 43920

East Palestine Branch
309 N. Market St.
East Palestine, OH 44413

New Philadelphia Branch
1433 SW 5th St.
New Philadelphia, OH 44663

Kent Branch
143 Gougler Ave.
Kent, OH 44240

Salem Branch
785 E. State St.
Salem, OH 44460

Lisbon Branch
966 ½ N. Market St.
Lisbon, OH 44432

Steubenville Branch
226 N. 4th St.
Steubenville, OH 43952

Medina Branch
704 N. Court St.
Medina, OH 44256

Graceworks Lutheran Services
www.graceworks.org/cccs
(800) 377–2432

Dayton Branch
3131 S. Dixie Dr., Suite 300
Dayton, OH 45439

Springfield Branch
204 N. Fountain Ave.
Springfield, OH 45504

Sidney Branch
113 N. Ohio St., Suite 202
Sidney, OH 45365

LifeSpan CCCS
www.lifespanohio.org
(888) 597–2751

Hamilton Branch
1900 Fairgrove Ave.
Hamilton, OH 45011

Middletown Branch
1001 Grove St.
Middletown, OH 45044

Lebanon Branch
1054 Monroe Rd.
Lebanon, OH 45036

Oklahoma

CCCS of Greater Dallas
www.cccs.net
(800) 944–3826

Ardmore Branch
333 W. Main St., Suite 150
Ardmore, OK 73402

CCCS of Central Oklahoma, Inc.
www.cccsok.org
(405) 789–2227
(800) 364–2227

Bethany Branch
3230 N. Rockwell Ave.
Bethany, OK 73008

Oklahoma City (South) Branch
5350 S. Western Ave., Suite 103
Oklahoma City, OK 73109

Enid Branch
317 W. Cherokee, Suite A
Enid, OK 73701

Shawnee Branch
130 E. MacAuthur
Shawnee, OK 74804

Lawton Branch
5202 SW Lee Blvd.
Lawton, OK 73505

Stillwater Branch
118 W. 8th Ave.
Stillwater, OK 74074

Oklahoma City (North) Branch
2525 NW Expy., Suite 660
Oklahoma City, OK 73112

Tinker AFB Branch
Bldg. 420
Tinker AFB, OK 73145

CCCS of Oklahoma, Inc.
www.cccsofok.org
(918) 744–5611
(800) 324–5611

Bartlesville Branch
117 W. 5th St., Suite 408
Bartlesville, OK 74003

Claremore Branch
104 S. Missouri Ave., Suite 205
Claremore, OK 74017

Broken Arrow Branch
317 S. Main St.
Broken Arrow, OK 74012

Muskogee Branch
323 W. Broadway, Suite 404
Muskogee, OK 74401

Sapulpa Branch
Community Resource Center
19 N. Main St.
Sapulpa, OK 74066

Tulsa Branch
4646 S. Harvard Ave.
Tulsa, OK 74135

Oregon

Money Management International
www.moneymanagement.org
(866) 889–9347

Albany Branch
214 NW Hickory St.
Albany, OR 97321

Eugene Branch
1200 High St., Suite 150
Eugene, OR 97401

Bend Branch
1010 NW 14th St., Suite 100
Bend, OR 97701

CCCS of Coos-Curry, Inc.
www.cccscoos.org
(800) 248–7040

Coos Bay Branch
375 S. 4th St., Suite 100
Coos Bay, OR 97420

CCCS of Josephine County
www.cccsgrantspass.com
(800) 365–6002

Grants Pass Branch
1314 NE Foster Way
Grants Pass, OR 97526

CCCS of the Tri-Cities
www.cccswaor.org
(800) 201–2181

Hermiston Branch
240 E. Gladys Ave., Suite 3
Hermiston, OR 97838

CCCS of Southern Oregon, Inc.
www.cccsso.org
(541) 779–2273

Klamath Falls Branch
740 Main St.
Klamath Falls, OR 97601

Medford Branch
820 Crater Lake Ave., #202
Medford, OR 97504

ClearPoint Financial Solutions, Inc.
www.clearpointcreditcounselingsolutions.org
(877) 422–9040

Portland Branch
9955 SE Washington St., Suite 301
Portland, OR 97216

Douglas CCCS
www.cccsdouglas.org
(800) 417–3104

Roseburg Branch
849 SE Mosher Ave.
Roseburg, OR 97470

CCCS of Mid-Willamette Valley, Inc.
www.cccssalemoregon.com
(503) 581–7301
(888) 254–8449

Salem Branch
1564 Commercial St. SE
Salem, OR 97302

Pennsylvania

CCCS of Delaware Valley
www.cccsdv.org
(800) 989–2227

Blue Bell Branch
1777 W. Sentry Pkwy., Suite 200
Blue Bell, PA 19422

Bristol Branch
1230 New Rodgers Rd., Suite F1
Bristol, PA 19007

Jenkintown Branch
261 Old York Rd., Suite 401
Jenkintown, PA 19046

Media Branch
280 N. Providence Rd., Suite 7
Media, PA 19063

Norristown Branch
113 E. Main St.
Norristown, PA 19401

Philadelphia (Center City) Branch
1608 Walnut St., 10th Floor
Philadelphia, PA 19103

Philadelphia (Chinatown) Branch
901-A Wood St.
Philadelphia, PA 19107

Philadelphia (North) Branch
4400 N. Reese St.
Philadelphia, PA 19140

Philadelphia (Northeast) Branch
7340 Jackson St.
Philadelphia, PA 19136

West Chester Branch
790 E. Market St., Suite 170
West Chester, PA 19382

Money Management International
www.moneymanagement.org
(866) 889–9347

Easton Branch
306 Spring Garden St.
Easton, PA 18042

Pottstown Branch
1954 E. High St.
Pottstown, PA 19464

Quakertown Branch
245 W. Broad St., Suite 3
Quakertown, PA 18951

Whitehall Branch
3671 E. Crescent Ct.
Whitehall, PA 18052

Wyomissing Branch
833 N. Park Rd., Suite 103
Wyomissing, PA 19601

Advantage Credit Counseling Service, Inc.
www.cccspa.org
(888) 511–2227

Altoona Branch
917A Logan Blvd.
Altoona, PA 16602

Butler Branch
112 Hollywood Dr.,
Suite 101
Butler, PA 16001

Erie Branch
4402 Peach St.
Erie, PA 16509

Greensburg Branch
1 Northgate Sq.
Greensburg, PA 15601

Harrisburg Branch
2000 Linglestown Rd., Suite 302
Harrisburg, PA 17110

Pittsburgh Branch
2403 Sidney St., Suite 400
Pittsburgh, PA 15203

York Branch
970-D S. George St.
York, PA 17403

CCCS of Northeastern Pennsylvania, Inc.
www.cccsnepa.org
(800) 922–9537

Bloomsburg Branch
702 Sawmill Rd.
Bloomsburg, PA 17815

Hazleton Branch
214 W. Walnut St.
Hazleton, PA 18201

Pittston Branch
401 Laurel St.
Pittston, PA 18640

State College Branch
202 W. Hamilton Ave.
State College, PA 16801

Stroudsburg Branch
411 Main St., Suite 104
Stroudsburg, PA 18360

Sunbury Branch
217 S. Center St.
Sunbury, PA 17801

Williamsport Branch
201 Basin St.
Williamsport, PA 17701

Tabor Community Services
www.cccscentralpa.org
(800) 788–5062

Lancaster Branch
308 E. King St.
Lancaster, PA 17602

CCCS of Northeastern Ohio
www.credit-counseling.org
(800) 355–2227

Grove City Branch
734 Stambaugh Ave.
Sharon, PA 16146

Rhode Island

Money Management International
www.moneymanagement.org
(866) 889–9347

Warwick Branch
501 Centerville Rd.
Warwick, RI 02886

South Carolina

Family Service Center of South Carolina
www.fsconline.org
(803) 773–5450

Camden Branch
United Way Bldg.
110 E. DeKalb St.
Camden, SC 29020

Columbia Branch
2712 Middleburg Dr.,
Suite 207-A
Columbia, SC 29204

Florence Branch
United Way Bldg.
1621 W. Palmetto St.
Florence, SC 29501

Orangeburg Branch
976 Middleton St., Suite 11
Orangeburg, SC 29115

Rock Hill Branch
150 Oakland Ave., Suite 229
Rock Hill, SC 29730

Sumter Branch
31 E. Calhoun St.
Sumter, SC 29150

CCCS of the Savannah Area, Inc.
www.cccssavannah.org
(843) 379–2227
(800) 821–4040

Beaufort Branch
69 Robert Smalls Pkwy.,
Suite 2B
Beaufort, SC 29902

CCCS of the Central Savannah River Area
www.cccsaugusta.org
(800) 736–0033

Graniteville Branch
560 Jefferson Davis Hwy.
Graniteville, SC 29829

Compass of Carolina
www.compassofcarolina.org
(800) 203–9692

Greenville Branch
1100 Rutherford Rd.
Greenville, SC 29609

Spartanburg Branch
145 N. Church St., Suite 120A
Spartanburg, SC 29306

Greenwood Branch
Turner House
123 Bailey Circle
Greenwood, SC 29649

Family Services, Inc.
www.fsisc.org
(800) 232–6489

Conway Branch
United Way Bldg.
761 Century Circle
Conway, SC 29526

Charleston (North) Branch
4925 LaCross Rd., Suite 215
Charleston, SC 29406

South Dakota

Lutheran Social Services of South Dakota
www.lsssd.org
(888) 258–2227

Aberdeen Branch
202 S. Main St., Suite 228
Aberdeen, SD 57401

Spearfish Branch
2519 Windmill Dr.
Spearfish, SD 57783

Brookings Branch
306 4th St., Suite C
Brookings, SD 57006

Vermillion Branch
816 E. Clark St.
Vermillion, SD 57069

Huron Branch
1371 S. Dakota Ave., Suite 202
Huron, SD 57350

Watertown Branch
1424 9th Ave., Suite 7
Watertown, SD 57201

Mitchell Branch
403 N. Lawler, Suite 206
Mitchell, SD 57301

Yankton Branch
610 W. 23rd St., Suite 4
Yankton, SD 57078

Sioux Falls Branch
705 E. 41st St., Suite 100
Sioux Falls, SD 57105

CCCS of the Black Hills
www.cccsbh.com
(800) 568–6615

Pierre Branch
209 E. Sioux Ave.
Pierre, SD 57501

Rapid City Branch
111 St. Joseph St.
Rapid City, SD 57701

Tennessee

Family Service Agency—CCCS
www.helpingfamilies.org
(501) 753–0202

Bartlett Branch
2855 Stage Village Cove, Suite 5
Bartlett, TN 38134

Memphis (Midtown) Branch
2400 Poplar Ave., Suite 445
Memphis, TN 38112

Partnership for Families, Children, and Adults, Inc.
www.partnershipfca.com
(800) 568–6615

Chattanooga Branch
1800 McCallie Ave.
Chattanooga, TN 37404

ClearPoint Financial Solutions, Inc.
www.clearpointcreditcounselingsolutions.org
(877) 422–9040

Clarksville Branch
1685 Ft. Campbell Blvd., Suite D
Clarksville, TN 37042

Memphis Branch
555 Perkins Rd. Ext., Suite 417
Memphis, TN 38117

CCCS of Middle Tennessee
www.credit-counseling.org
(800) 355–2227

Cookeville Branch
225 N. Willow Ave., Suite 343
Cookeville TN, 38501

Nashville Branch
1101 Kermit Dr., Suite 204
Nashville, TN 37217

Murfreesboro Branch
201 E. Main St., Suite 100
Murfreesboro, TN 37130

Nashville (Belle Meade) Branch
4525 Harding Rd., Suite 211
Nashville, TN 37205

CCCS of Greater Atlanta
www.cccsatl.org
(800) 251–2227

Johnson City Branch
2112 N. Roan St., Suite 706
Johnson City, TN 37601

Maryville Branch
523 W. Lamar Alexander Pkwy.,
Suite 1
Maryville, TN 37801

Knoxville Branch
531 Callahan Dr., Suite 101
Knoxville, TN 37912

Money Management International
www.moneymanagement.org
(866) 889–9347

Kingsport Branch
1999 E. Stone Dr., Suite 102
Kingsport, TN 37660

Texas

Money Management International
www.moneymanagement.org
(866) 889–9347

Abilene Branch
500 Chestnut, Suite 1511
Abilene, TX 79602

Burleson Branch
1161 SW Wilshire, Suite 116
Burleson, TX 76028

Beaumont Branch
5825 Phelan Blvd., Suite 102
Beaumont, TX 77706

East Harris County Branch
12605 East Freeway, Suite 500
Houston, TX 77015

Bedford Branch
4001 Airport Freeway,
Suite 520
Bedford, TX 76021

Fort Worth Branch
1320 S. University Dr.,
Suite 200
Fort Worth, TX 76107

Bryan/College Station Branch
3833 S. Texas Ave., Suite 275
Bryan, TX 77802

Fort Worth (North) Branch
2100 N. Main St., Suite 224
Fort Worth, TX 76106

Fort Worth (Southeast) Branch
Southeast YMCA Bldg.
2801 Miller Ave.
Fort Worth, TX 76105

Houston (Fuqua) Branch
11550 Fuqua, Suite 350
Houston, TX 77034

Houston (Greenway) Branch
1 Greenway Plaza, Suite 130
Houston, TX 77046

Houston (West) Branch
4600 Hwy. 6 N, Suite 250
Houston, TX 77084

Houston (Whitney Bank) Branch
1716 Mangum
Houston, TX 77092

Houston (Willowbrook) Branch
7915 FM 1960 W, Suite 240
Houston, TX 77070

Humble Branch
125 W. Main St.
Humble, TX 77338

Killeen Branch
1711 E. Central Texas Expy., Suite 302
Killeen, TX 76541

Lake Jackson Branch
122 West Way, Suite 407
Lake Jackson, TX 77566

Lubbock Branch
3223 S. Loop 289, Suite 416
Lubbock, TX 79423

Lufkin Branch
2718-B S. Medford Dr.
Lufkin, TX 75901

Mansfield Branch
1275 N. Main St.,
Suite 101–2
Mansfield, TX 76063

Odessa Branch
2626 JBS Pkwy., Suite B-103
Odessa, TX 79761

San Angelo Branch
3115 Loop 306, Suite 102
San Angelo, TX 76904

Southlake Branch
1500 Corporate Circle, Suite 6
Southlake, TX 76092

Spring (The Woodlands) Branch
25025 I-45 N, Suite 525
Spring, TX 77380

Stafford Branch
12603 SW Freeway, Suite 625
Stafford, TX 77477

Texas City Branch
2501 Palmer Hwy., Suite 250
Texas, City TX 77590

Waco Branch
6801 Sanger Ave., Suite 202
Waco, TX 76710

CCCS of Greater Dallas, Inc.
www.cccs.net
(800) 249–2227

Amarillo Branch
6300 W. Interstate 40, Suite 106
Amarillo, TX 79106

Arlington Branch
Chase Bank
1600 E. Pioneer Pkwy., Suite 345
Arlington, TX 76010

Austin Branch
1106 Clayton Ln.,
Suite 490W
Austin, TX 78723

Corsicana Branch
200 N. 13th St., Suite 208
Corsicana, TX 75110

Dallas Branch
8737 King George Dr.,
Suite 200
Dallas, TX 75235

Dallas (North) Branch
14110 Dallas Pkwy., Suite 280
Dallas, TX 75254

Dallas (North Park) Branch
6500 Greenville Ave., Suite 440
Dallas, TX 75206

DeSoto/Lancaster Branch
1229 E. Pleasant Run Rd., Suite 214
DeSoto, TX 75115

Duncanville Branch
402 W. Wheatland Rd.,
Suite 116
Duncanville, TX 75137

Garland Branch
3960 Broadway Blvd., Suite 115
Garland, TX 75043

Irving Branch
4322 N. Belt Line Rd.,
Suite B-207
Irving, TX 75038

Longview Branch
Texas Bank and Trust
1800 W. Loop 281, Suite 201
Longview, TX 75604

Mesquite Branch
3939 US Hwy. 80 E,
Suite 323
Mesquite, TX 75150

Richardson Branch
Chase Bank
100 N. Central Expy., Suite 320
Richardson, TX 75080

Tyler Branch
1001 E. Southeast Loop 323, Suite 250
Tyler, TX 75701

Waxahachie Branch
Comerica Bank
820 Ferris Ave., Suite 375
Waxahachie, TX 75165

Wichita Falls Branch
4210 Kell Blvd., Suite 200
Wichita Falls, TX 76309

Budget & Credit Solutions
www.debt.org
(888) 880–6337

Austin Branch
505 E. Huntland Dr.,
Suite 440
Austin, TX 78752

CCCS of South Texas
www.cccsstx.org
(800) 333–4357

Brownsville Branch
634 E. Levee St.
Brownsville, TX 78520

McAllen Branch
221 Nolana, Unit B
McAllen, TX 78504

Corpus Christi Branch
1706 South Padre Island Dr.
Corpus Christi, TX 78416

Victoria Branch
3908-A John Stockbauer Dr.
Victoria, TX 77901

Harlingen Branch
2202 S. 77 Sunshine Strip, Suite C
Harlingen, TX 78550

CCCS of North Central Texas, Inc.
www.cccsnct.org
(800) 856–0257

Carrollton Branch
1925 E. Belt Line Rd.,
Suite 453
Carrollton, TX 75006

McKinney Branch
901 N. McDonald St.,
Suite 600
McKinney, Texas 75069

Denton Branch
4094 S. Summerhill, Suite 202
Denton, TX 76201

Plano Branch
101 E. Park Blvd., Suite 757
Plano, TX 75074

Texarkana Branch
4094 Summerhill Sq.
Texarkana, TX 75503

CCCS of Greater San Antonio, Inc.
www.cccssa.org
(800) 410–2227

Del Rio Branch
1927 Bedell Ave.
Del Rio, TX 78840

Kerrville Branch
Wells Fargo Bank
222 S. Sidney Baker St.,
Suite 204
Kerrville, TX 78028

Laredo Branch
5415 Springfield, Suite 2A
Laredo, TX 78041

San Antonio Branch
6851 Citizens Pkwy., Suite 100
San Antonio, TX 78229

San Antonio (Universal City) Branch
1001 Pat Booker Rd.,
Suite 201
Universal City, TX 78148

San Antonio (South) Branch
Bank of America Bldg.
111 Rayburn Dr.
San Antonio, TX 78221

San Marcos Branch
300 S. CM Allen Pkwy.,
Suite 200B
San Marcos, TX 78666

Seguin Branch
516 Jefferson Ave.
Seguin, TX 78155

Uvalde Branch
216 W. Main St.
Uvalde, TX 78801

CCCS of the YWCA—Paso Del Norte Region
www.ywcaelpaso.org
(888) 533–7502

Katherine White Harvey Branch
313 Bartlett Dr.
El Paso, TX 79912

Joyce Whitfield Jaynes Branch
1600 Brown St.
El Paso, TX 79902

Myrna J. Deckert Branch
9135 Stahala Dr.
El Paso, TX 79924

Lower Valley Branch
115 Davis Dr.
El Paso, TX 79907

Shirley Leavell Branch
10712 Sam Snead Dr.
El Paso, TX 79935

Utah

CCCS of Southern Nevada & Utah
www.cccsnevada.org
(800) 451–4505

St. George Branch
720 S. River Rd., Bldg. C-235
St. George, UT 84770

Vermont

CCCS of New Hampshire & Vermont
www.cccsnh-vt.org
(800) 327–6778

Barre Branch
84 S. Main St.
Barre, VT 05641

Burlington Branch
31B Swift St.
South Burlington, VT 05403

Brattleboro Branch
81 High St.
Brattleboro, VT 05301

Rutland Branch
26 West St.
Rutland, VT 05701

Virginia

Money Management International
www.moneymanagement.org
(866) 889–9347

Alexandria Branch
801 N. Pitt St., Suite 117
Alexandria, VA 22314

Fairfax Branch
3927 Old Lee Hwy., Suite 101E
Fairfax, VA 22030

Collinsville Branch
4846 Kings Mountain Rd.
Collinsville, VA 24078

Leesburg Branch
604 S. King St., Suite 007
Leesburg, VA 20175

Manassas Branch
10629 Crestwood Dr.
Manassas, VA 20109

Roanoke Branch
7000 Peters Creek Rd.
Roanoke, VA 24019

ClearPoint Financial Solutions, Inc.
www.clearpointcreditcounselingsolutions.org
(877) 422–9040

Charlottesville Branch
1658 State Farm Blvd., Suite B
Charlottesville, VA 22911

Chesapeake Branch
1417 N. Battlefield Blvd.,
Suite 295
Chesapeake, VA 23320

Colonial Heights Branch
3701 Boulevard, Suite D
Colonial Heights, VA 23834

Danville Branch
139 Deer Run Rd., Suite A
Danville, VA 24540

Dumfries Branch
17119 Wayside Dr.
Dumfries, VA 22026

Fort Lee Branch
3105 A Ave.
Fort Lee, VA 23801

Fredericksburg Branch
2217 Princess Anne St.,
Suite 322
Fredericksburg, VA 22401

Newport News Branch
728 Thimble Shoals Blvd.,
Suite A
Newport News, VA 23606

Richmond (Bells Road) Branch
4605 Commerce Rd.
Richmond, VA 23234

Richmond Branch
8000 Franklin Farms Dr.
Richmond, VA 23229

Staunton Branch
1600 N. Coalter St.,
Suite 18B
Staunton, VA 24401

Virginia Beach Branch
522 S. Independence Blvd.,
Suite 103
Virginia Beach, VA 23452

CCCS of Hampton Roads
www.debtfreeonline.com
(757) 826–2227

Hampton Branch
2021 Cunningham Ave.,
Suite 400
Hampton, VA 23666

Washington

CCCS of Yakima Valley
www.cccsyakima.org
(800) 273–6897

Ellensburg Branch
309 E. Mountain View Ave.
Ellensburg, WA 98926

Wenatchee Branch
230 Methow St.
Wenatchee, WA 98801

Moses Lake Branch
821 W. Broadway St.
Moses Lake, WA 98837

Yakima Branch
1115 W. Lincoln, Suite 119
Yakima, WA 98902

Sunnyside Branch
911 E Edison Ave.
Sunnyside, WA 98944

ClearPoint Financial Solutions, Inc.
www.clearpointcreditcounselingsolutions.org
(877) 422–9040

Everett Branch
2731 Wetmore Ave., Suite 200
Everett, WA 98201

Seattle Branch
9709 NE 3rd Ave., Suite 210
Seattle, WA 98115

Kent Branch
841 North Central, Suite C-213
Kent, WA 98032

CCCS of Olympic-South Sound
www.credit-counseling.org
(800) 355–2227

Bellevue Branch
12505 Bel-Red Rd., Suite 109
Bellevue, WA 98005

University Place Branch
3560 W. Bridgeport Way
University Place, WA 98466

Olympia Branch
2102-A Carriage Dr.,
Suite 102
Olympia, WA 98502

Vancouver Branch
1325-B Officers Row
Vancouver, WA 98661

CCCS of the Tri-Cities
www.cccswaor.org
(800) 201–2181

Kennewick Branch
401 N. Morain
Kennewick, WA 99336

Walla Walla Branch
5 W. Alder St., Suite 240
Walla Walla, WA 99362

CCCS of Northern Idaho
www.cccsnid.org
(800) 556–0127

Pullman Branch
350 SE Fairmont Rd.
Pullman, WA 99163

Money Management International
www.moneymanagement.org
(866) 889–9347

Spokane Branch
4407 N. Division, Suite 814
Spokane, WA 99207

West Virginia

CCCS of Southern West Virginia
www.cccswv.com
(800) 281–5969

Beckley Branch
111 Lebanon Ln.
Beckley, WV 25801

Charleston Branch
1219 Ohio Ave.
Dunbar, WV 25064

Logan Branch
201 ½ Stratton St.,
Suite 407
Logan, WV 25601

Teays Valley Branch
3983 Teays Valley Rd., Suite 101
Hurricane, WV 25526

Criss-Cross, Inc.
www.criss-crosswv.org
(800) 498–6681

Clarksburg Branch
209 W. Pike St., Suite B
Clarksburg, WV 26301

Morgantown Branch
1299 Pineview Dr., Suite 3
Morgantown, WV 26505

CCCS of the Mid-Ohio Valley
www.wvcccs.org
(866) 481–4752

Parkersburg Branch
2715 Murdoch Ave., Suite B4
Parkersburg, WV 26101

Ravenswood Branch
910 Washington St.
Ravenswood, WV 26164

St. Marys Branch
213 Washington St.
St Marys, WV 26170

Goodwill Industries
www.goodwillhunting.org
(888) 534–4387

Huntington Branch
1102 Memorial Blvd.
Huntington, WV 25701

Wisconsin

CCCS of Beloit/Janesville
www.cccsbeloit.org
(608) 365–1244
(866) 925–2227

Beloit Branch
423 Bluff St.
Beloit, WI 53511

Janesville Branch
205 N. Main St.
Janesville, WI 53545

Catholic Charities of La Crosse
www.catholiccharitieslax.org
(888) 212–4357

Eau Claire Branch
448 N. Dewey St.
Eau Claire, WI 54703

Prairie du Chien Branch
115 E. Perry St.
Prairie du Chien, WI 53821

La Crosse Branch
3710 S. East Ave.
La Crosse, WI 54601

Wausau Branch
401 S. 5th St., Suite 235
Wausau, WI 54403

Marshfield Branch
101 W. 29th St., Suite 103
Marshfield, WI 54449

FamilyMeans
www.familymeans.org
(800) 780–2890

Eau Claire Branch
2194 EastRidge Center
Eau Claire, WI 54701

CCCS of Greater Milwaukee
www.creditcounselingwi.org
(888) 799–2227

Elkhorn Branch
22 S. Wisconsin St., Suite 4
Elkhorn, WI 53121

Milwaukee (South) Branch
4915 S. Howell Ave., Suite 102
Milwaukee, WI 53207

Milwaukee (West) Branch
10400 W. North Ave., Suite 495
Milwaukee, WI 53226

Whitefish Bay Branch
4650 N. Port Washington Rd.
Milwaukee, WI 53212

Waukesha Branch
101 W. Broadway
Waukesha, WI 53186

FISC—A Program of Goodwill Industries
www.fisc-cccs.org
(800) 366–8161

Green Bay Branch
1660 W. Mason St.
Green Bay, WI 54303

Sturgeon Bay Branch
30 N. 18th Ave., Bldg. 1
Sturgeon Bay, WI 54235

Manitowoc Branch
4335 Calumet Ave.
Manitowoc, WI 54220

Waupaca Branch
805 W. Fulton St.
Waupaca, WI 54981

Menasha Branch
921 Midway Rd.
Menasha, WI 54952

Wisconsin Rapids Branch
2561 S. 8th St.
Wisconsin Rapids, WI 54494

Oshkosh Branch
1600 W. 20th Ave., Suite 140
Oshkosh, WI 54901

GreenPath Debt Solutions
www.greenpath.com
(800) 550–1961

Madison Branch
802 W. Broadway, Suite 202
Madison, WI 53713

Milwaukee (Greenfield) Branch
4811 S. 76th St., Suite 317
Milwaukee, WI 53220

Credit Counseling Centers of Wisconsin
www.cccofwi.org
(800) 350–2227

Fond du Lac Branch
131 S. Main St.
Fond du Lac, WI 54935

Sheboygan Branch
1930 N. 8th St., Suite 100
Sheboygan, WI 53081

La Crosse Branch
311 A Main St.
La Crosse, WI 54601

West Bend Branch
139 N. Main St., Suite 101
West Bend, WI 53095

Lutheran Social Services of Minnesota
www.lssmn.org
(888) 577–2227

Superior Branch
2231 Catlin Ave.
Superior, WI 54880

Money Management International
www.moneymanagement.org
(866) 889–9347

Kenosha Branch
8600 Sheridan Rd.
Kenosha, WI 53143

Racine Branch
420 7th St.
Racine, WI 53403

Wyoming

CCCS of Northern Colorado and Southeast Wyoming
www.cccsnc.org
(800) 424–2227

Cheyenne Branch
2113 Warren Ave.
Cheyenne, WY 82001

Index

Possessions. *See* property;
property, personal
Post-filing problems, 125
Property. *See also* home; land;
property, personal; vehicles
auctioning of, 87–88
audits of, 146
in Chapter 13 bankruptcy,
134–135, 138
judgment liens against, 23–24
loss of, 62
paid-off, 70
protection of, 23, 62–70 (*See
also* exemptions)
risk of losing, 87
and secured debts, 40
seizure of, 23
selling of to family or friends,
111–112
threats of seizure of, 16–17
Property, personal
protection of, 47
valuation of, 48
Proposed plan, 136–137
Protection. *See also* exemptions
from creditors, 20
of home, 44–45, 86
of nonpurchase money
security items, 41
of property, 23, 62–70
of real estate, 46
of vehicles, 46–47, 86–87

Q
Quick debt ratio, 36–40

R
Reaffirming debt, 106–107,
118, 151–153, 164
Real estate. *See also* home;
property
protection of, 46
Refinancing, 73–74
Rent, 31–32
Reorganization, plan of,
130–131
Reports, independent, 129
Repossession, 25–26, 40, 62, 134
Restitution payments, 44
Retirement savings
borrowing against, 52–53, 55,
76
potential crisis in, 7
protection of, 49

S
Savings. *See* emergency fund;
retirement savings
Section 341 meeting, 119–123
Self-employment. *See also* small
business owners
and difficulty in finding loans,
168
and rebuilding credit, 155, 158
Separation after bankruptcy,
142–143
Shame, 12
Shot gunning, 167
Small business owners. *See also*
self-employment
lack of specialized bankruptcy
for, 100

About the Authors

Wendell Schollander received his BA in economics and his MBA from the Wharton School of Finance at the University of Pennsylvania. He received his law degree from Duke University. Mr. Schollander has practiced law in the corporate and bankruptcy fields for more than thirty years. He has served as general counsel of RJR Archer and the Specialty Tobacco Counsel. Mr. Schollander currently practices law in Winston-Salem, North Carolina.

Wes Schollander received his BA from the University of North Carolina and his JD from Wake Forest School of Law. He is a member of the North Carolina Bar Association and the North Carolina Young Lawyers Association. Mr. Schollander currently practices law in Winston-Salem, North Carolina.